The Father
– of –
GLACIER
NATIONAL PARK

*Discoveries and Explorations
in His Own Words*

GEORGE BIRD GRINNELL
Compiled by Hugh Grinnell

Foreword by John Taliaferro

THE
History
PRESS

Published by The History Press
Charleston, SC
www.historypress.com

First published 2020

Manufactured in the United States

ISBN 9781467143240

Library of Congress Control Number: 2019954283

CONTENTS

FOREWORD

By 1885, George Bird Grinnell was a seasoned westerner and a committed conservationist.

He'd spent his boyhood on the wooded shore of Manhattan Island, on an estate that once belonged to wildlife artist John James Audubon. After his graduation from Yale in 1870, he postponed working for his father on Wall Street and instead accompanied paleontologist Othniel Marsh and a group of classmates on a fossil-digging expedition on the Great Plains. Conveniently, the transcontinental railroad had been completed a year earlier, making it possible for adventurers like Grinnell to commute, if you will, from coastal cities to the American outback with comparative ease. For the next fifteen years—indeed for the next fifty—Grinnell made seasonal migrations westward, hunting buffalo with the Pawnees, penetrating the Black Hills with George Armstrong Custer's Seventh Cavalry (an intrusion that eventually led to Custer's comeuppance at the Little Bighorn) and surveying an overland trail across Montana, from the Missouri River to "the national park," Yellowstone, in 1875. In 1883, he bought a ranch in the Shirley Basin of southern Wyoming. He could ride and rope and shoot. He could cinch the diamond hitch. He had fought prairie fires. He had faced Indians on the warpath.

During these years, Grinnell had matured in another way, too. Where initially he had regarded the "frontier" as a tableau embroidered on the romantic pages of James Fenimore Cooper, Francis Parkman or (his favorite) Mayne Reid, he had come to recognize a larger, more sobering saga unfolding before his eyes. The dinosaur bones that he and his Yale chums dug up provided a graphic lesson in evolution and extinction. Likewise, he could not ignore the impending disappearance of the great bison herd—once numbering more than thirty million—that, until recently, had carpeted the vast grasslands. And the Plains Indians: could their extinction be far off, now that their sovereignty was reduced to reservations, and the pantry of protein on which they depended was being destroyed solely for its hides or, worse, out of sheer spite? Grinnell was many things—author, editor, outdoorsman—but he was everlastingly a naturalist. He painstakingly chronicled the wild lands and wildlife he explored in his seasonal rambles. His leather-bound diaries are crammed with penciled field notes of bird species and their habitats, big game in its haunts. And once he took ownership of the gentleman's sporting journal *Forest and Stream*, its black-and-white columns were increasingly devoted to natural history and the cause of protecting the nation's forests and streams, mountains and prairies, from ill-considered diminution and destruction. In October 1879, Grinnell issued a grim forecast for the West's future:

> *As I look back on the past ten years and see what changes have taken place in these glorious mountains* [he meant the Rockies in general] *I can form some idea of the transformations which time to come will work in the appearance of the country, its fauna and its flora. The enormous mineral wealth contained in the rock-ribbed hills will be every year more fully developed.... Towns will spring up and flourish, and the pure, thin air of the mountains will be blackened and polluted by the smoke vomited from the chimneys of a thousand smelting furnaces; the game, once so plentiful, will have disappeared with the Indian; railroads will climb the steep sides of the mountains and wind through the narrow passes, carrying huge loads of provisions to the mining towns, and returning trains will be freighted with ore just dug from the bowels of the earth; the valleys will be filled with fattening cattle, as profitable to the owners as the mines are to theirs; arable land will be taken up and cultivated, and finally the mountains will be stripped of their timbers and will become simply bald and rocky hills. The day when all this shall have taken place is distant no doubt, and will not be seen by the present generation; but it will come.*

As Hugh Grinnell notes in his introduction, George Bird Grinnell was eulogized by the *New York Times* as "the father of American conservation." Deservedly so. At the risk of sacrilege, let us acknowledge that neither Henry

David Thoreau nor John Muir, for all their exemplary conduct and enduring eloquence, ever strode the halls of Congress and the Interior Department or drafted legislation to preserve public lands and vulnerable creatures. Grinnell founded the first Audubon Society. With Theodore Roosevelt, Grinnell convened the Boone and Crockett Club to preach the ethics of "fair chase" to their fellow big-game hunters. It was Grinnell, through persistent lobbying and editorializing, who perceived that the national park—and eventually all national parks—could be something beyond mere "pleasuring grounds" for the public and ought to serve as wildlife preserves as well. The alarm he sounded against the poaching of buffalo in Yellowstone arguably spared the species, which by 1890 had been reduced to a remnant of roughly one or two hundred, from joining the passenger pigeon and the Carolina parakeet on the list of the forever lost. Speaking of birds, his stubborn labor on behalf of the first federal Migratory Bird Protection Act of 1913 would anticipate the Endangered Species Act sixty years hence.

But let us reset the calendar to 1885. Grinnell's appetite for adventure had not been slaked over the previous decade and a half. Nor was his memory dimmed. The invasion of the Black Hills, first by Custer and then by rapacious gold miners, had left an indelible impression. More recently he had observed firsthand the greedy mitts of railroads and other commercial rackets on the crown jewels of Yellowstone. When James Willard Schultz, a New Yorker who married a Blackfeet woman and settled on the reservation in northwest Montana, invited Grinnell to poke around in what, by Schultz's depiction, promised to be a more pristine corner of the continent, the thirty-five-year-old naturalist-Nimrod jumped at the chance. "He arrived on the mail stage," Schultz recalled of their first meeting, "a slender, quiet, fine appearing man of medium height, in outing clothes that showed much use; his baggage a canvas-covered bedroll, a war sack, a Sharps .45 caliber rifle, and a fly rod. No tenderfoot he."

—John Taliaferro

John Taliaferro is the author of *Grinnell: America's Environmental Pioneer and His Restless Drive to Save the West*

AUTHOR'S NOTES

B ird" Grinnell was a prolific writer and record-keeper. When in camp after a long day's hunt or exploration, he diligently made time to "do this work"—in other words, record his and his group's daily activities. He knew before traveling to Montana that he would write a series of articles about each trip for publication in *Forest and Stream*, so he was deliberate in detailing his activities. However, since his daily sojourns required hours of being away from camp, his limited time upon returning to camp often provided him with little remaining daylight—or worse, only firelight—to record his daily entries. On rainy days, he took advantage of his "down" time to update his journal. On occasion, because of returning to camp tired, wet and hungry, he would need to wait a day or two before finding time to write. As a result of these inconveniences, in his journals are many run-on sentences—a series of "and then," "and therefore," "but we" and so on. To make this book more readable, the author has eliminated many of the conjunctions in his journals and his published articles and has made shorter sentences by adding needed punctuation marks. In addition, in keeping with the first-person journal entries that comprise approximately 50 percent of this book, many third-person pronouns from published articles will be changed to first person for the reader's benefit. After all, George Bird Grinnell is telling his own story.

Bird Grinnell, a name he preferred and was first used by his Yale classmates, studied Greek and Latin as a student. After a western expedition in 1872, he wrote an article about a buffalo hunt with the Pawnee that he signed *Ornis*, which is Greek for "bird." He walked it to the offices of *Forest and Stream* in New York City, his hometown, to deliver it. He often rode horseback with the Pawnee Indian scouts who provided protection for the 1870 Yale student expedition. He learned a few words of Pawnee and "was disposed to learn more." Later on, after a trip in 1873 to Wyoming and Colorado, he began using a different pseudonym, *Yo*, for his *Forest and Stream* articles. He probably learned "Yo" from the wagon driver, Joe (Jose Alleyo Felemanches). "Yo" means "I" in Spanish, and Bird used "Yo" often in his published articles as a nickname rather than indicating the first person.

IN HIS DAILY JOURNALS, Bird often interchanged "S." for James Willard Schultz. "Appekunny" is Schultz's Blackfeet name. "Yellow Fish" is the translation of Charlie Rose's Blackfeet name, "Otu Komi." "Brocky" is the nickname (or possibly American surname) of Tail-Feathers-Coming-In-Sight-Over-The-Hill. Grinnell also spelled words as he heard them. *St. Mary's* River is actually *St. Mary* River; *Appekunny* is spelled Apikuni by the Blackfeet; *Swift Current* has generally been accepted as one word; *Pegunny* is Pikuni in Blackfeet; Kootenai (or sometimes Kutenai) is spelled as he heard it: *Kootenay*. I deferred to his spelling in the story.

ALL OF THE MAPS featured here are by Carla Majernik, taken from *Grinnell's Glacier* by Gerald A. Diettert, Mountain Press Publishing Company, 1992. On these maps, Carla Majernik located and drew rivers, streams and major lakes. The author added mountain locations and names, exploration trails, names of lakes and explanatory notes.

THIS BOOK CONTAINS MANY hunting and fishing stories from the nineteenth century, before the park was created and before hunting and fishing regulations were established for the park. Sportsmen should contact the National Park Service to obtain current regulations before attempting to hunt or fish within the park boundaries.

INTRODUCTION

There have been several very good books written about George Bird Grinnell. Authors usually tell a story composed of approximately 95 percent author's prose and commentary and 5 percent quotes by, or about, the person who is the subject of the book. This book is different in that 90 percent of the story is taken from the writings of George Bird Grinnell—essentially a storyteller telling his own story. Only 10 percent is author's commentary or extracts from important references.

"Geo. Bird Grinnell" (the way he signed his name due to his preference to be called "Bird") was a prolific writer. He was a contributor to *Forest and Stream* sportsmen's weekly journal and later the editor and owner. As editor, he wrote his weekly editorials, taking on issues of high importance to the American public. He also wrote many series of articles about his travels and expeditions, and these were scientific, humorous, romantic, detailed, graphic, picturesque, imaginative and more. He maintained an ongoing correspondence from the 1870s until his death in 1938 with literally dozens of friends from his time in the American West and Canada. Many readers wrote letters addressed to "Editor, Forest and Stream," and he maintained contact with these writers. None of these letters went unanswered. The Yale University Library Archives houses many boxes—dozens of linear feet—of his correspondence due to his habit of making onionskin copies of all his outgoing letters.

In other books written about him, George Bird Grinnell is often *spoken about* or *referred to*. Using his correspondence, editorials, three multi-article series of Montana expedition articles in *Forest and Stream*, daily expedition journals and references about him in national magazines, journals and books, the author has developed a story told by Grinnell himself, which allows the reader to feel as if he/she actually accompanied him on his daily marches through northern Montana. It will feel to the readers as if they are sitting around the after-dinner campfire listening to the explorers summarizing the day's activities. Before his Montana treks began, Bird had become generally interested in the American West. He was lured to Montana when he received two articles from James W. Schultz, a New Yorker turned Blackfeet Indian, to be published in *Forest and Stream*. The articles described the multitude of game animals and different species of lake and stream fish. He was "hooked" and made plans to visit Montana in 1885 and to hire the author of the articles to be his guide. He brought his Sharps rifle and a fly rod, intending to experience this mecca for the outdoorsman. By the time his month in Montana was completed, he dreamed not only of returning to hunt and fish but also of revisiting a glacier he and his two companions had discovered.

This story depicts the daily activities of his almost yearly expeditions in the late nineteenth century prior to beginning the effort to preserve this area as a national park. There are hunting successes and failures; campfire talks and stories; packhorses falling into streams and horses missing in the morning; discoveries named for Indians, hunting companions and great Americans; plenty of rain, cold, fog and snow. Readers need to tightly tie their boots and wear parkas while reading about these discoveries.

After reading this book, the reader will have come to know a great American who was called the "Father of American Conservation" by the *New York Herald Tribune*. He founded the first Audubon Society and co-founded the Boone and Crockett Club with Theodore Roosevelt where he was named "President for Life" in 1927. He received the Theodore Roosevelt Medal for Distinguished Service in 1926. On that occasion, in his presentation remarks, President Calvin Coolidge told Grinnell: "The Glacier National Park is peculiarly your monument." In 1910, when President William H. Taft signed the bill that created the park, it became the "Park for all Americans."

1

1885

Hunting and Fishing in the St. Mary's Lakes

The steps which led to the establishment of the Glacier National Park have already been forgotten by most people. That, after all, is not important. The great thing is that this beautiful region has been saved for the public.
—George Bird Grinnell, 1914

~The names affixed to glaciers, mountains, and lakes all had specific meaning, not only to him and his small group of explorers, but to the Blackfeet who lived there.

In 1885, George Bird Grinnell made his first visit to the area that was to be an annual destination for nearly forty years. He left New York in August and, after a week's pause in Yellowstone, took the Northern Pacific train to Helena. Then Grinnell took a mail stage and rode 116 miles farther to Fort Benton, where he was met by James Willard Schultz, a young New Yorker, who, in 1877, had left his home to work for his uncle in St. Louis but found himself drawn to adventure in the West. He had taken a riverboat with some trappers up the Missouri River to Montana and eventually worked for Joe Kipp at a trading post near the Blackfeet Nation and married into the Piegan tribe in the Small Robes band. Schultz began to write about his life as an Indian and sent articles to Forest and Stream, an outdoorsman's weekly journal for which GBG had been the editor since 1876. Schultz submitted an article titled "Hunting in Montana," which Forest and Stream published in 1880, and another titled "To Chief Mountain," which was published in 1885. The articles spoke of hunting for mountain sheep and goats and fishing for huge trout, among stupendous mountains surrounded

Left: James Willard Schultz. *Butterfly Lodge Museum, Greer, Arizona. Right*: Joseph Kipp. *Wikimedia.*

by walled-in lakes, and was the reason Grinnell finally made this trip. In one of his later books, Schultz described Grinnell as "a slender, quiet, fine-appearing man of medium height; in outing clothing that showed much use; his baggage a canvas-covered bedroll, a war sack, a Sharp's .45 caliber rifle, and a fly rod. No tenderfoot he, we thought."[1]~

September 1 and 2

We left the Piegan [tribe of the Blackfeet Confederacy] Agency for the Walled-In Lakes, so the Piegans have named the bodies of water which form the source of the St. Mary's River. Our party was not a large one. It consisted of Schultz (named "Appekunny" by the Piegans), Yellow Fish and Yo.[2] Yellow Fish, also known as Charlie Rose, is a French half-breed, but one

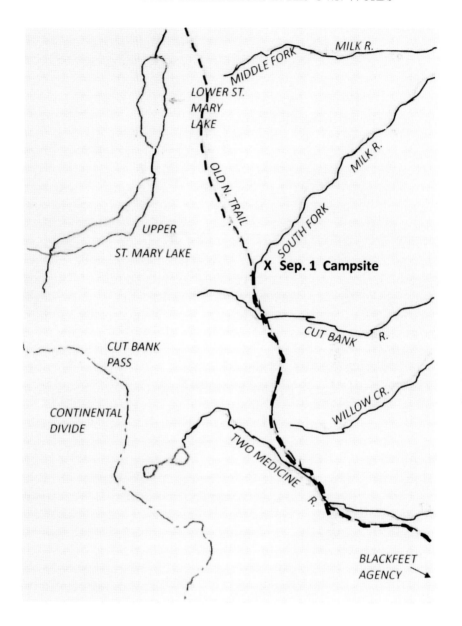

who has always lived with his mother's people. He can speak only a very few words of English. We were starting on a short trip to the St. Mary's Lakes.... Our wagon held a...10x10 wall tent and a sheet iron cook stove, with our bedding and provisions which completed the load in the wagon. Our arms comprised a rifle apiece, and Mr. Schultz had also a shotgun....I had a light split bamboo fly-rod.

15

For the first forty-five miles of the distance from the agency to the lakes there is a wagon road, but at Milk River, named by the Lewis and Clark Expedition because of its turbid, white color, it is necessary to turn off from this and follow up the stream for some distance toward the mountains, and then…to travel northwest toward the St. Mary's.[3]

So far we had driven in the wagon which contained our outfit, but at Cut Bank we were to get a couple of saddle horses. Mine was an old buffalo horse, tough and wiry, and steady under fire, and Appekunny's was a little blue, quite spirited, but somewhat run down by hard work. After turning out the team horses I set up my rod, and with Appekunny, who carried his shotgun, strolled off up the creek and began to cast for trout.… As the fly fell lightly on the water on the further edge of a pool, there was a simultaneous movement on the part of several of the shadows which made it certain that they had life, and a second later a fine trout was fast to the tail fly. [He made] the rod bend as I tried to keep him out from the sunken root which he at once tried to reach. Here we took half a dozen fish, none of them over a pound in weight.[4]

September 3

Started at eight. While cooking breakfast we had a fine view of the mountains lying on the other side of St. Mary's Lake—which the Indians call The Walled-In-Lakes.[5]

Lower lake is from 6 to 8 Mi. long and upper somewhat longer. Each about 1 mile from widest parts.…Though St. Mary's R is bent almost at right angles about ⅓ the way back from its outlet, lower ⅔ nearly E&W. It is walled in on either side by mts of great height & steepness and has no valley except at the lower end.[6]

It rained during the night and things in the morning were a little wet. [We t]ravelled up Milk River for a mile or two and then turned off up a wide creek valley on the upper part of which were some elk sign. Saw five [wild] chickens (S. killed 3) and ducks and a wolf about noon.…It began to rain and soon a cold mt. storm was upon us. We were drenched before camp was made but after dinner felt more comfortable. Loaded shells in the afternoon. It snowed a little toward night. Camped about one o'c on little willowing creek.…Pine comes down nearly to our camp. During quite a long talk tonight, Rose said that in old times the Blackfeet owned all the country north of Belly River. The place for goats is on the upper lake.

St. Mary's Lake. *Author photo.*

He says the buck goats camp far apart for they are great fighters among themselves. Often you find them with round holes in their ribs, made by the sharp pointed horns of their opponents.[7]

That evening Yellow Fish…had something to say about Eh-mah-kee-kinny (big horn [sheep], or literally in Piegan, big head) and Ah-pah-mah-kee-kinny (white goat, literally white head). They [bighorn sheep] were on almost all the rough mountains except those on which the goat lives. The best place for these [goats] is on the west side of the upper lake on a great mountain where there are no sheep.…What I have so briefly summarized he told with a great deal of detail, and the hour was late when the talk ended and we were ready to turn in. A glance outdoors showed that the rain had turned into snow which was coming down softly and slowly and melting as it fell. No signs of clearing weather were visible in the sky.[8]

SEPTEMBER 4

On looking out this morning we found the ground covered with snow to a depth of four or five inches. As soon as it stopped snowing we packed up and about 9:30 we pulled out. Yellowfish and I were in the lead and Appekunny driving the team behind us....The lower hills are covered with quaking aspen which gradually change into pines towards the tops of the ridges which are only 1500 to 2000 feet higher. The character of the upper lake is quite different. Here most magnificently the majestic mountains come down in steps almost sloping on the natural cut walls to the water's edge, and the lake is very deep from its shore. These lakes are evidently glacial in their origin, and here and there in the ravines are to be seen great masses of snow which suggest the presence of a few small glaciers still remaining in the sheltered spots.[9]

When the wagon came up there was some question as to whether it would be wise to make the descent into the basin at this point....By means of a couple of log-chains we prepared the wagon as well as possible for the somewhat perilous descent. The mere upsetting and scattering of our goods and chattels over the hillside would have been no great misfortune, but if the wagon once got away from us on this very precipitous slope, it seemed likely that it would not stop before the bottom of the hill was reached. In this case we should not only have the wagon to mend, but very likely also a dead horse to leave behind. So with one man managing the reins and brake, and two behind trying to keep the hind end of the wagon from sliding down the hill, we started very carefully and slowly....The slope was a hard grass-covered gravel, and over this were two or three inches of snow and ice. The rough-locks, instead of catching, slid along over the ground like the runners of a sleigh. Do the best we could, Yellowfish and I were hardly able to keep the wagon from swinging around and starting down the hill backward. Little by little, however, we worked our way down and as soon as possible edged the wagon into a grove of aspens where it was impossible for it to get away. Then by cutting a path with the axe we managed to safely reach the foot of the steep hill....We gradually worked down the slopes until we came to a curving bay near the head of the lake where we made camp. It was a pleasant spot, open and level....A few yards down the beach, hidden among the alders, we found Appekunny's boat, undisturbed during the ten months that had elapsed since he cached it there. Under it were the oars, thole pins [fulcrums for oars] and guff, and in a few moments we had launched and brought it to the end of the path

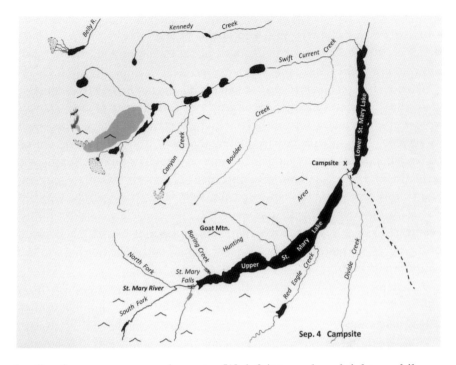

leading from our camp to the water. We left it to soak and tighten while we went back to camp.

After dinner, taking rifle, rod, and trolling lines, we set forth to paddle up the lake to the inlet. Yellowfish was loath to accompany us, for the Piegans do not like to venture upon the water. They know that terrible gods—the underwater people—live down in the bottoms of these lakes, and they fear Windmaker and the others. Similarly many of the west coast Indians fear to venture on the mountain lakes, dreading the power of the monsters that inhabit them, and in this fear we see another example of a belief that is worldwide among savage people. After some persuasion he was induced to come.[10]

September 5

With Rose, I started about 6:45 to climb a mountain for sheep. The day was dark and threatening…and a heavy mist, which lifted now and then, hid the sides of the mountains. We hoped, however, that the weather might improve. After riding 3 or 4 miles and crossing the stream which joins the two lakes, we began the ascent on horseback, riding through the quaking aspen groves and climbing the steep slopes. At length we came to the place where we had to leave our horses and begin toiling on foot through the snow and over the rocks....[11]

The top of the slope reached, we had left all vegetation. Before us nothing was to be seen but a wide expanse of gray rock and white snow which ran up to a vertical cliff whose top was hidden in the dense mist....It was impossible to see more than fifty or sixty feet in any direction, and hunting was out of the question. Any game that was not moving rapidly would be sure to see us before we saw it....A keen wind was blowing and with the drenching fog had by this time made us both very cold. Yellowfish's toes were sticking out of his torn moccasins, and I was wet up to my knees. The cold damp mist penetrated to one's very marrow. We spent an hour or two by this boulder, tramping up and down and beating our arms against our sides in fruitless efforts to keep warm.

At length, seemingly disgusted, the Indian said, "Let's go home." I made an assenting gesture and he led the way down the slope....Just before dark we reached camp—wet, tired, and hungry.[12]

SEPTEMBER 6

A diabolically severe tramping after sheep with Schultz & Rose. No game seen.[13]

SEPTEMBER 7

While I was hammering away at the wretched coffee, which very obstinately refused to be ground, I turned over in my mind what we had better do during the day. I felt rather too stiff to undertake another day on the mountains and determined to just loaf about camp all day long. In theory loafing is a most delightful way of passing the time, but in practice it fails to satisfy. As long as one has something to potter over—some pretense of an occupation—he does very well. But after the rifle is wiped and the frayed silk on the middle joint of the rod neatly whipped, the rents in clothing mended and the broken strings replaced on the saddle, he becomes uneasy. A pipe or two, smoked as he reclines stretched out at full length on his blankets, fails to soothe, and he rises, walks out of doors, stretches in the warm sunshine, yawns, and then concluded that he must do something.

About the middle of the morning S. and I walked up to the inlet. He carried his shotgun and I my rod. Crossing to the main stream we saw the fresh tracks of a moose and later we could see that a few moose habitually come down to the inlet to feed and water. It seems likely that they come down from the mountains at night and return again toward morning.[14]

As we crossed the little stream within a short distance of the camp, a ruffed grouse hopped from the ground in front of us into the lower limbs of an alder, where she sat not six feet distant and looked at us. There was at once a division of opinion as to what course should be pursued with the game. On the one hand it was suggested that the bird's head should be promptly shot off. Against this it was urged that she was ragged and almost featherless and had probably just reared a brood, and this being the case she would not be fit to eat. Except for food it was not worthwhile to kill her. The bird sat there like a judge and listened with great gravity to both sides of the argument, but as she said nothing it is presumed that she reserved her decision. We could not agree as to what should be done and so passed on, leaving the bird sitting there turning her head from side to side as if somewhat perplexed by the reasons that had been offered on both sides.…

Retracing our steps we killed a widgeon on our way to camp, dined early, and then tried still-fishing for lake trout.… [B]eing unsuccessful at this, [we] set a net for whitefish. We had just finished this operation and rowed back to the shore, when we saw a horseman appear over a ridge a mile further down the lake, and could see even at this distance that he was an Indian. Before he had advanced fifty yards toward us he began to ride in circles along the hillside. Yellowfish called out, "He is drunk," to which I responded, "No, he is signaling." This proved to be the case, for a little later, when the Indian stopped at the camp to talk, he said that he was informing some of his companions who were in sight, but out of hearing, that he had discovered some people. He was a Kootenay but could talk some Piegan and told us that eight lodges of his people under the chief, Back-In-Sight, were camped some miles below on the river. They had been out fifty days and had been quite successful in their hunting, having killed about forty sheep, two bears—one black and one grizzly—one moose, a few elk, and plenty of beaver. Their main business was trapping, and they hunted only when meat was required for the camp.…There were still sheep on the mountains, but they were high up among the rocks, and it was hard to get to them.…So chatting about the game and the country, we sat in front of the tent until the sun had set. Then the Kootenay clambered onto his steed and rode away into the shadows.[15]

SEPTEMBER 8

Just after breakfast 4 Kootenays, including the one who called last night and who can talk Piegan, came to camp and talked and smoked for a while. S. & I left them here while we saddled up and went down to the outlet.…In the St. Mary's River below the lakes we caught a few fish.…After fishing for a while here, two Kootenay riding one horse appeared on the opposite bank of the river and inquired by signs where their camp was. One of them was a man with whom Schultz had talked by sign language at the agency and they were evidently just from there.…A little later on we stopped fishing and went up the river to where the trail crosses.…We rode across the broad bottom toward the Indian camp.…The Kootenay camp consisted of 8 lodges, and they must have had 75 head of horses, most of them very fine ponies. The camp was clean, and the people seemed well to do. All the men were out hunting, but the women were quite pretty for Indians. Staked out on the ground were the skins of sheep and a black bear. Hanging on trees [were] the skin of a large grizzly, a dressed moose skin, and numerous bundles of dried sheep meat. We did not stop long in the camp nor speak to any of the people except one or two boys. They said that there were plenty of fish in the creek, and we went down to it, set up the rod, and caught a few. Returning to camp as it was growing late, we killed a few more dusky grouse on the quaking aspen ridges. This is most delightful sport. The birds are large and strong of wing and get up with a swish of wing that quite equals that of a partridge.… At night after we had eaten supper, four Kootenays rode into camp, each with a sheep on his saddle. This fairly made me foam at the mouth with rage and envy. They said that they had killed them on a mountain east of the upper lake, which we at first supposed to be this inaccessible mtn but which afterwards proved to be the one back of it. One of the Kootenays said that he would come next day and hunt with us.[16]

SEPTEMBER 9

About 10 o'c two young Kootenay boys came to camp to hunt with us.… We therefore started at once—Rose, the Kootenays and I. S. said he would rather remain in camp. The boys started at once on a gallop and before crossing a creek running into inlet turned up toward the rocks on E side of upper lake.…At length we reached a point where it was necessary to leave the horses, and then a 15-minutes steep climb up a very slippery slope brought us to the point where we might expect to see sheep.…Sheep tracks were seen everywhere in the soil and some of them were extremely fresh, but no game was seen. After looking about for a little, the biggest Kootenay boy started off to try to start some game and drive it to us. Rose perched himself on a rock, and the younger Indian and I cowered behind a big rock a little lower down. I took quite a fancy to this boy who was quite young and very full of mischief. As we were both very cold and shivering I passed him the pipe for which he seemed very grateful. It snowed constantly and blew with gusto, violence, and was very cold.…At length Rose, frozen out, went down into the ravine and started a fire about which we gathered and got a little warm. In a couple of hours the boy in blue returned and said that there were plenty of sheep sign on the other side of the mountains but that the clouds and snow were so thick that he could not see any.[17]

We went back to the horses and, cold and wet, began the descent of the mountain. This was even more disagreeable than the climb up had been, for now we had not hope to sustain us.…The only incident that varied the monotony of this climbing was a tumble which I had. Jerry [my horse,] was larger than the Indian ponies and not nearly so agile, and in attempting to follow the boys up the side of a very steep ravine he tumbled over backward. When I felt him going I jumped from the saddle, and horse and rider rolled down the steep bank side by side. Neither suffered any injury, but I was very well pleased that I had got out of the saddle in time to avoid being struck by the horse.…I then followed the tracks of the boys until I overtook them at the edge of the timber. In camp that night after dinner I was grumbling at the bad luck which seemed to follow us, which was due largely to the wretched weather.

September 10

The next day two Kootenays…rode up to the camp and proposed to go hunting. No one seemed to care to go except myself, and so saddling Jerry, we were soon on the way toward the mountain which we had first climbed, the one on the westside of the upper lake. As I rode along behind the Kootenays I rather wondered how I should communicate with them in case I should have anything special to say.…A good deal could be said by signs, but I am not especially proficient in this language, and there is always a chance for a misunderstanding of the particular sign on which the sense of the whole communication depends.[18]

On the way to the mountain I explained to the Indian that I was a poor climber and that they would have to go slowly to have me keep up. To this he seemed to agree, but, when we came to the mountain, he and his comrade started off and soon left me far behind. When I got to the point of the mt. they were nowhere in sight....Soon it began to snow and blow and was very cold. I performed my customary operation of sitting on a rock and shivering. During one snow squall a sheep snorted somewhere above me on the steep mt. wall, but the snow was so thick that I could not make it out. After perhaps an hour and a half I heard three shots up the canyon, and after some debating in my mind I started off to where the reports came from. After going a mile or more I stopped to look and listen, and as I was standing there I saw the head of a sheep appear, coming toward me over a ridge. It was walking, but it discovered me at the same time I saw it and stopped. I had slowly sunk down by a big rock as soon as I saw it. It had evidently been alarmed by the shooting and after pausing a moment started to run by me on the upper side. Twice it stopped, once at about 200 yds and once at 100, and then ran swiftly by. Both times it stopped I tried to shoot, but the snow blew so thickly that I could not see the sights on my rifle. A third time it stopped, this time at about 150 yds and behind a pile of rocks so that I could see only its head and neck. I knew that it was now or never, so I fired. The wild bound that the animal gave and the fact that it started at headlong speed down the hill assured me that my shot had told. Springing from rock to rock I hurried to a point where it had passed along. Some spots of blood on a little patch of snow told the story, which the wide spread hoof marks in the loose shale confirmed. The trail was an easy one to take and I followed it at a half run down the mountain side. Once or twice where the creature had made a little turn I ran [past the trail], but a glance backward always gave it to me again. As I went on, the blood was more abundant, and soon I felt sure that the sheep must be found within a short distance. A little farther was a patch of low willows a foot or two in height over which a broad smear of blood ran, and looking beyond them down over a ledge 12 or 15 feet high I saw the game stretched on its side. It was quite dead. It proved to be a yearling ewe, probably the best and sweetest meat I could have killed.[19] (Ed: The Schultz story, which appeared in his book *Signposts of Adventure*, is a fiction. Schultz and Yellow Fish were back in camp and never were present when Bird shot the ewe, not a "ram with horns the size of wash tubs." Grinnell told Schultz the story when he returned to camp after hunting with the Kootenai. Schultz was a storyteller—a good one—but he changed the details from 1885 when his book was published in 1926.) The problem arose while I was butchering as to how I was to get my meat to where the horses were. The distance was perhaps three miles and necessitated a climb of perhaps 1500 feet...and then a descent of about 2000 ft. to the horses. The sheep would weight dressed from 80 to 100 pounds. While butchering [it], I kept hoping that the Indians would come along and I could get them to carry the meat, but they did not come. If we had had any meat in camp I would have taken only the hams and saddle that I could perhaps have carried. As no help came, however, I finally threw the animal on my back and began the ascent of the mountain. It was a frightful climb, hard enough when I had only myself to carry, and now weighed down by the load of meat and my gun, it seemed at first as if it would be impossible for me to go 100 yards. By frequently stopping to take a breath, I at last made about half the ascent. Then placing the beast on a high rock sat down and took a good long rest. Once when going slowly along over the loose tipping rocks I fell, and it seemed to me as if a dozen holes had been punched in my ribs and all my limbs broken, but I was getting mad now and so shouldering my burden again I pushed on. I rested—that is threw off my load—four times during

Singleshot Mountain. *Author photo.*

the journey, and at length, reaching the top of the long steep hill, I could see the horses. Down this hill I dragged the sheep and while doing so saw behind me the Indians bowed down beneath loads of meat. I supposed that they had each killed a sheep, but I soon saw that they had but one between them so that really their loads were lighter than mine had been. Packing the meat on the horses we were soon at the camp where my load was gladly welcomed. When I detailed to Schultz the circumstances of my shot, he proposed to call the mountain where [the shot] had been made "Singleshot Mt." It is the great buttress-like mountain west of the lower end of the upper lake.…The Kootenays…crossed [my] trail and asked me [how I] had made it.…[T]hey asked me if it was a good trail and if I would not lead them down by it. So I rode ahead and led them to our camp. This tickles me, guiding Kootenays about through their own mountains!

September 11

We have concluded tomorrow to move down to the lower end of the lake. A white man named Dick King is camped there, and he will watch our camp while we go to the Goat Mt.—a two-day's trip.…Got packed and away by 10 o'c and started down the lake having cached the boats & oars. On the way down…I found 3 blue-winged teal in a little slough & killed two on the water and the third as he flew. The wagon crossed the St. Mary's R. before I got there and when opposite the camp Rose made me a sign which I supposed meant to cross there. I started in, and the water grew deep pretty rapidly, but I supposed that I had reached the deepest part when suddenly the old horse plunged off into a hole and began to swim. I had got up as high as possible on the saddle, but of course got wet now up to my waist. A few yards of swimming brought Jerry to his footing, and I landed. The scene caused great amusement to all hands in camp. We had six or eight Indians to dinner, but they only got what we left. In the evening S. & Rose went to Kootenay camp, but I stayed here to finish this work [of recording the days' events].

September 12

Started about 7 o'c with pack horse for the narrows of Upper St. Mary's Lake where the sheep are said to be abundant and goats are found. We carried bedding and some bread and salt.…About the time we passed our

Author photo.

old camp at the head of the lake it began to rain…and from there to the narrows it stormed violently all the time. We got pretty wet up to the knees. We got to camp about 12. The pack had fallen off once in crossing a stream through the brush, and the bedding was somewhat damp. [After lunch] we at once started out to hunt, Rose taking the south end of Singleshot Mt and S. and I the W. end of Goat Mt. We hunted faithfully for about 3 hours. No fresh sign of any kind was seen, and there was no evidence of any game having been in the vicinity for months.…By this time we were all pretty wet and so [continued] on to our own camp which we reached in about four hours, probably about 8:30—cold, wet & hungry.… [I addressed Yellowfish:] "Well, friend, Yellowfish, though you had bad luck, your hunt was not all for nothing. That little stream you followed up to where it heads, we name for you. From now on it is Otokomi (Yellowfish) Creek and next north of it is Otokomi Mountain." I named the basin in which lay the lake "Rose Basin" for Charlie Rose.

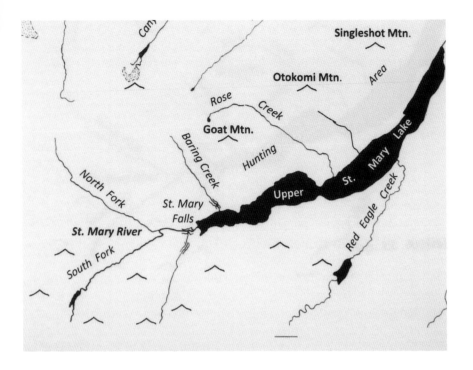

SEPTEMBER 13

S., King, & Rose have gone to the end of the lower lake to bring down boat. R.&K. [brought] back the horses they rode. We shall probably go to Swift Current in a day or two, another [day] back to agency....About 4 o'c Dick returned [to camp] having sailed nearly all the way down the lake.[20]

[After King returned, Appekunny and I joined him to fish for lakers.] We had rowed perhaps a mile when King, who was in the stern of the boat, gave a wild wave of the arm which held his trolling line. It tightened for a moment, and a heavy swirl appeared in the water fifty feet in our wake. Then the line suddenly yielded and came in without resistance. A few seconds later my rod bent, and I struck the fish so hard that Appekunny gave a cry of caution: "Look out, or you'll smash your rod." But I had unlimited confidence, born of past experience, in the tough bamboo, and I wanted to set the hook fast. I did so. The fish did not at first make off as they usually do but remained for a few seconds nearly in the same place while he shook himself so furiously that I feared he would throw the steel out of his jaws. Then he made one or two short, fierce rushes [and once broke water] but after that seemed to give up the fight. Slowly I brought him to the surface at the boat's stern, and just as the gaff was put into him we could see why he had yielded so easily. In his shaking, when first struck, he had wound the line several times about his head, and his gills were fast bound down so that it was impossible for him to breathe. He was a small fish, only weighing four pounds, but from his stomach we took a couple of young whitefish five or six inches long, with which we replaced our baits of fish belly. And always after that we looked for these fry in the lake trout that we caught, and invariably found one or more. They are the most taking bait for these fish that we discovered.[21]

The wind, which rose again as the sun set, was cold, and as soon as dinner was over we took refuge in the lodge. Sticks were thrown on the smoldering coals of the fire, and Yellowfish, seizing the axe, went out and cut a couple of armfuls of wood which he brought inside and laid by the door. By this time the pipes and cigarettes were all aglow, and the fire gave out a cheerful warmth which made the howling gale without, a thing to be laughed at. We lay back on our comfortable beds, with our feet stretched out toward the fire, and were just lazy and contented. It was too soon after dinner to talk, and we quietly enjoyed the warmth and listened to the raging of the wind [as we] sent up clouds of fragrant tobacco smoke.[22]

September 14

…We were today to start on a two days' excursion to the Swift Current Lakes, and then having seen them and the mountains about them, to return to St. Mary's and then to depart for the Agency. [The Blackfeet words to describe these lakes mean "swift-flowing river." I called it "Swift Current."] It happened that I rode down last into the water and just before me was the pack horse which Yellowfish was leading.…I was close behind the pack horse which hung back, and rode out of the water above the trail.…Just as I had got clear of the water I saw the pack horse rear as if to put his feet on the [steep] bank and then fall over backward, nearly pulling Yellowfish out of the saddle. The beast fell squarely on the pack, and the force of the current swept him along, rolling him over half a dozen times, giving him another turn every time he tried to regain his feet until, at length, exhausted, he lay still with nothing but his head and half the pack out of the water. By this time we were all off our horses and down by the water's edge. Yellowfish ran into the stream and caught the lariat, and we dragged the dripping beast to shore and up the bank. From every corner of the pack the water was trickling in capacious streams, and it was plain that our bedding was well-soaked.…

The pack was jerked off the saddle and its contents exposed. The blankets were wrung out and spread in the sun to dry, and the damp bread treated in like fashion. Then we sat down and while the horses fed and the blankets dried, we grumbled....So we [ate] a couple of the damp biscuits, and I gave Appekunny a piece of tobacco....We smoked and waited for an hour or two longer, when the things having become a little dry, we packed up and started on.

We rode over a little ridge in view of the lower of the Swift Current Lakes. These lakes were discovered a few years ago by a hunting party and have been visited only once or twice by white men. They have been reported as being five in number. [As they had not been named, I and my companions simply called them "First Lake," "Second Lake" and so on.] The lower one is perhaps a mile in length and quite broad. Those above it are smaller but still quite considerable. The water of Swift Current [Creek] is markedly different in one respect from that of most mountain streams. These are usually pure and as transparent as crystal. Swift Current, however...is pale greenish, and its aspect...led me to suspect the existence of glaciers at the head of the stream....

As we advanced, the confines of the valley drew closer and closer together, and the mountains became more abrupt. Finally on the north they became mere vertical walls of from three to four thousand feet in height.... At intervals of a mile or less, narrow canyons opened out from between the mountains, leading back into wide amphitheatre-like basins scooped out in time long past by the action of the ice. On the south side of the stream, the mountains, though seemingly less steep, were higher....As we advanced and could see further up the valley, a superb glacier came into view. It lies on the south side of the stream and forms the source of a sixth lake which is an arm of the fifth, which has, until now, been considered the uppermost of the Swift Current Lakes.

We made camp below Fifth Lake in a little patch of green timber—it being thought that further up the stream there would be found no grass for the horses."[23]

~Fifth Lake was referred to as Swift Current Lake by Grinnell in 1885 but became known as Lake McDermott a few years later for an old-time lumberman who built a lumber mill in the area. In 1929, the name Swiftcurrent Lake was restored at the insistence of Superintendent Eakin because "Mr. McDermott's sole contribution to the Park was despoiling its forests."[24]~

Before doing anything else, Appekunny and I went up the trail to see the falls at the outlet of Fifth Lake, for we had heard them described in glowing

Five Lakes, Swiftcurrent Valley. Lakes in foreground not yet discovered. *Louis Hill, Minnesota Historical Society.*

terms as being one hundred feet high and of great beauty. We were greatly disappointed in them. They consist of a series of broken cascades, each about twenty-five feet high, the stream itself being about twenty feet wide and flowing between vertical walls of rock. The lake itself, walled in as it is by lofty mountains, is very beautiful. From an elevated point we could see

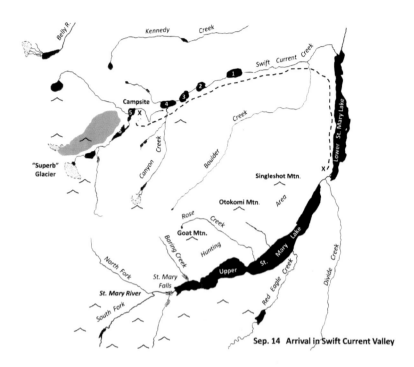

Sep. 14 Arrival in Swift Current Valley

something of a sixth lake, the greater part of which was concealed behind a great mountain. The waters of this lake are green and milky—true glacier waters, in fact—and a well-defined line in the fifth lake shows where its clear waters and the milky ones of its arm come together. Very impressive is the superb mountain which lies between [the] fifth and sixth lake[s], and partially conceals the glacier which gives origin to the latter.…Behind this mountain and over sixth lake the glacier was visible. We could see at least a mile of its width, and how much was hidden from view we could not conjecture.…The thickness of this mass of ice we estimated at several hundred feet, but as our efforts to reach it were unsuccessful, we can only guess at this.

Our fire that night was built in a little opening among the spruces, and as it burned high after dinner the tips of the overhanging boughs crackled sharply in the heat. On sticks set in the ground about [camp] were our damp garments smoking in the warmth. The tent strung on a rope between two convenient trees stood a few yards back from the fire, and as I surveyed the camp from my couch of dry pine needles on the opposite side of the fire, it had a wonderful, comfortable and homelike aspect. Even an old dweller like myself is sometimes surprised by the very little it requires to make a comfortable home in the wilderness. Blankets and fire are all that is needed. You can really carry your home about with you on your saddle.…

Fifth Lake and Falls. *National Park Service.*

Unnamed glacier. *USGS 1914, Marble photo.*

Our talk that night was of the superb mountains about us, of the great ice masses that furrow their side, and of the possibilities of meat for the morrow. As we talked, the wind howled down the valley and made curious sad murmurs through canyon and ravine, while the tops of the spruces tossed themselves to and fro, sighing in an undertone that was but faintly heard. Our fire burned bravely upward, for where we were the wind could not reach us, and it was warm and bright and pleasant. The pipes kept going well; there was plenty of wood; we lounged about and chatted or dozed until at length one by one we crept into our blankets and the wind sang our lullaby.[25]

SEPTEMBER 15

Long before the sun had made his appearance over the high mountains we were astir. Our simple meal was soon finished, and Yellowfish at once started off on foot alone. A little later Appekunny and I departed up the trail, and the camp was left in charge of the dogs and horses. I was extremely anxious to get to the ice on the other side of the stream....Following the trail to the fifth lake (Ed: Bird sometimes referred to Fifth Lake as "the fifth lake" in his journal.) we went down to the water's edge and scanned the landscape to see how most readily we could reach our goal. By crossing the creek just back of camp and clambering for several miles along a very rough and precipitous mountain side, we could reach Fifth Lake at a point where only its width would separate us from the great glacier which overhangs it....We kept on up the trail until we had gone some little distance beyond Fifth Lake, and then crossing a game trail which branched off toward the stream, followed it in the hope of finding a crossing....The climbing was difficult, for the ledges rose one above another in a seemingly interminable series. We would clamber up one, almost hand over hand, and then having reached a little bench, follow it until some place was found where the next wall above us could be scaled....About every half hour it would rain or snow with great violence, and during such times we would shelter ourselves as best we could beneath some projecting rock and start on whenever the rain stopped....

During a lull in the storm and a gleam of sunshine, we had, from the highest point which we reached, a true view of Fifth Lake and those above it....The green color of the waters of the glacial lake (the sixth lake) is due to the grinding to powder by the slowly-moving ice mass of the green slates, shales, and schist which form so large a proportion of the mass of these

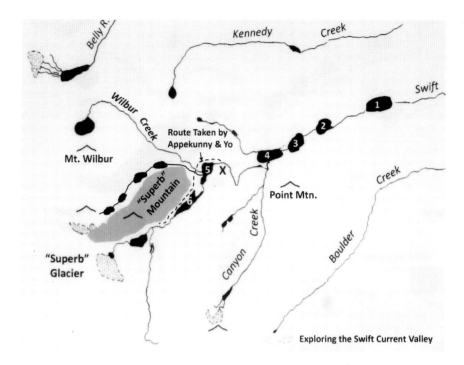

Exploring the Swift Current Valley

mountains. This finely comminuted rock is carried down by the water of the melting glacier and for some little time held in suspension by it, giving the water its peculiar tinge....Down the mountain side we slowly picked our way, and at dark, tired, hungry, wet and without game, reached the camp. There we found Yellowfish who had been in since noon. Soon after starting out, he said, he had got among goats and had shot away all his ammunition, twenty rounds, at them without getting one. He said that they had been very plenty [*sic*], and it was very amusing to hear him tell how, when he would shoot at one, it would jump down out of sight behind the rocks, and another would pop out from behind some other point to see what the noise was about. He said that he had hit several, but all too far behind, so that they got away among the rocks, and he could not find them.

Our provisions consisted of a small piece of bacon and four biscuits, and unless fresh meat could be obtained on the morrow, we should be obliged to return to the St. Mary's. Soon after supper my companions turned in, but I lay long by the fire, watching through the branches the stars in the sky, and listening to the soft whispers of the wind in the treetops and the distant murmur of the rushing stream.[26]

35

SEPTEMBER 16

There was little to be done about camp next morning. There was nothing to eat, and the preparations for breakfast consisted in whittling up a pipeful of tobacco apiece. While smoking, we changed the horses to fresh grass, and then shouldering our rifles started off for Point Mountain, which I had named. This had been Yellowfish's hunting ground of the day before. It was but a short walk to the rocks....Appekunny, who had set out with rubber boots on, was obliged to give it up and turn back. Yellowfish and I kept on and did some of the most difficult mountain climbing that I have ever undertaken....

The climbing was exceedingly difficult, and either from this cause or else because I had had nothing to eat that morning, I became very tired....After sitting down and smoking a pipe, I told him to go on. He trotted off and I followed at my best pace, which was, after all, a pretty slow one. By the time we had reached the level, snow-covered flat...I was fairly tired out. It was not...that I could not get my breath, but my legs from the waist down seemed almost incapable of motion. Even when walking on comparatively level ground I could advance only a few steps at a time without stopping and resting....Here we passed over another lake, this one frozen and its clear surface swept bare of snow by the bitter wind. We named the lake after Appekunny's wife, Natahki. Before we had made half the ascent to our present altitude it had begun to snow hard with a furious wind, and it was bitter cold. My shoes, much dilapidated by contact with the rocks, had gone to pieces during the morning, and when my weight broke through the crust of the snow field over which we were passing, the ice cut my feet....

As we neared the crest of the mountain I made better progress....At last it was accomplished, and we stood on the very crest of the mountains and looked directly down on the valley and the lakes and the stream. From the crest I viewed a mountain beyond Swift Current Lake with a majestic look which I named Mt. Wilbur for Edward R. Wilbur, long the Treasurer of Forest and Stream Publishing Company.[27]

Down in the valley the sun was bright and clear, and the stream gleamed and shone like a broad band of polished metal....Going down the hill... we walked upon a couple of blue grouse, one of which flew a few yards and alighted on the bare rocks. The other went into a little clump of pines. The former, Yellowfish killed; the latter, we could not discover. The bird was carried down to camp, and long before it was cold, [it] was roasting over the hot fire and was soon devoured. There being nothing more to eat in camp

Point Mountain. Point Mountain was later renamed Altyn Mountain by the miners who lived in the town of Altyn. Now Mount Wynn. *Author photo.*

Mount Wilbur. *Author photo.*

we packed up our possessions and started for the St. Mary's Lakes. As we rode down the valley in the bright sunlight I turned back for a last view of the stupendous mountains which we were leaving, but the dark snow clouds hung heavy over them and their rugged magnificence could not be seen.

SEPTEMBER 17

…The following day was occupied in fishing [on St. Mary's Lake] for lake trout and lounging about camp.…Yellowfish told us a story while we smoked our pipes. The story told and duly applauded, we turned into our blankets and were soon asleep.

SEPTEMBER 18

There were signs that the party's bad luck would cause its disruption. All the morning Yellowfish, Achilles-like, sulked in his tent, and a little after noon he saddled his horse, forded the river, and disappeared over the bluffs on his way to the agency. [Appekunny and I] spent the morning on the water fishing for lake trout, of which we caught fifty or sixty pounds' weight.…

This was to be our last night on the lakes, and it was marked by an incident which, for a short time, caused us some little uneasiness.…Two of the horses had disappeared and could not be found.…As the sun set, I asked…if the horses had been found. Appekunny replied that he and King had hunted everywhere but could not find them and that they had probably been stolen. Here was a pretty mess. Jerry was in sight, and the missing animals were those of the men who had been looking for them. I jumped on Jerry and set out to look for the missing beasts myself. By this time it was quite dark, but the great full moon, which had just climbed up over the eastern hills, cast over the plains a flood of white light.…In riding about, I depended much more on my horse's than on my own senses, and beyond keeping him in the general direction I wished to follow, interfered with him very little.…I had gotten within a couple of hundred yards of camp when I saw Jerry's ears prick and his head turn to the left, and by closely looking in the same direction, I made out two indistinct dark shapes, close under the shadow of the willows. As I rode toward them, a low whinny told me that I had found the missing horses. After riding close enough to recognize them I left them quietly feeding and went on to camp. I had been gone just twenty minutes.

September 19

The next day we said farewell to the Walled-In-Lakes, and leaving Dick King, the sole white inhabitant of the beautiful valley, set out across the river and up the steep bluffs....Late in the afternoon I had killed one of two sharp-tailed grouse that had shown themselves above the grass, and at dusk, while we were unharnessing, three mallards alighted in the pool at our feet. Appekunny very cleverly brought one of them to bag, so our supper and breakfast were provided.

September 20

...We started about 7:30 and had a long, quiet, uneventful day. A few miles before reaching Cut Bank we came to a little creek, already mentioned, in which were a great many ducks. Here Appekunny left his team in my charge and had some very pretty shooting, killing in a short time a dozen or fifteen teal, shovellers, and mallards....

When we reached Cut Bank, we found it for the time quite a busy place. Mr. Kipp, Major Allen, the Doctor, Mr. McGonigle, and two or three others had come out from the agency to have a day's fishing and were just going back. The latest news from the States was given us, and pretty soon the teams drove off while we made ourselves comfortable in John's cabin.

September 21

The next morning, after fruitlessly fishing for an hour or two, we started for the agency. While still some distance north of Two Medicine Lodge Creek, we noticed several single Indians riding about over the prairie as if looking for a trail. At length one of them rode near enough to us so that Appekunny made to him the sign of interrogation: What is it? or What is the matter?... To this the Indian replied, "Many horses stolen" and told us that during the night some Indians had run off 150 to 200 head of horses from the camp....All the Piegans who had any horses left were now out looking for the trail....We saw about twenty-five Indians riding in a body on the crest of the ridge on the other side of the valley....They had found the trail.... The opinion was freely expressed that [the thieves] would not be overtaken. They had twelve hours start and had all the best horses in the camp and a never-ending series of remounts. Besides, if the Piegans should catch them, it was thought very doubtful that they could recapture their property, for the Crows are well-armed, while the Blackfeet are not—many of the latter still being without guns....

That night we spread our blankets in the trader's store and enjoyed the kind hospitality of Mr. Joseph Kipp, while with Mr. McGonigle, a friend of many years' standing, I talked over the days and the men of early times.[28]

SEPTEMBER 22, 1885

The morning after our arrival at the Agency, we sent over to old Red Eagle, the most potent of the medicine men of the Pegunny, to ask him if he would unwrap the Bear Pipe for us. Red Eagle is a relative of Appekunny....Word came back from the old man that three hours before sunset he would be ready for us....I sat down on a log near the lodge and began to make friends with the small children....There was one little fellow about two years old who quite won my heart by his genial smile and general air of cordiality. His clothing consisted of several strings of beads, a buckskin thong about the neck, and an extremely abbreviated shirt which came down to his lower ribs. The rest of his person was covered only by a thick coating of mud....

At length Appekunny called me, and with him I entered the lodge in which were already seated a number of Indians. Red Eagle sat at the back with the fire between himself and the door, and at his left was a space where, in the place of honor, we seated ourselves....

~The ceremony took almost two hours, with prayers, singing, and passing the Bear Pipe among those who occupied his lodge....At the end of the ceremony, Red Eagle made a sign that the ritual was over, and they filed out of the lodge.[29]~

SEPTEMBER 23

The next morning as we were sitting in the trader's store, old Nei-SU Ki-YU [Four Bears], the camp orator, came in and began to tell us about the pursuit of the horse thieves by the Pegunny....All this Four Bears explained at great length and with such expressive gestures that I caught the sense of what he was saying even though I did not comprehend his word....Going into the store I got a plug of tobacco, which I put in my pocket. As I came out again Four Bears asked Mr. Kipp who I was, and he replied that I came from the end of the world, from the edge of the salt water. After a little more talk Four Bears said, "Come, I will give him a name."…[Then he faced me toward the sun and said:] "This is what you are called—Pi-nut-o-YE Is-tsim-o-KAN" [Fisher Cap, a hat made from the skin of a fisher—like a small wolverine].…I gave Four Bears the tobacco, which he accepted very pleasantly, and when, after a little further conversation, he learned that I was going to write down an account of it, he expressed a desire to write his name in my notebook. This he did by making his mark.

Our stay at the agency drew to a close, and late one afternoon we bade a cordial farewell to all those who had been so kind to us, and Appekunny and I drove off over the level valley, climbed the long hill, and turning, took our last view of the interesting spot. Then a few days later I bade farewell to Appekunny and started for the East. I had spent but a short time at the Wall-In-Lakes, and had accomplished but little in the way of shooting and fishing, yet I felt that the long journey had been well worth taking.…Of the marvelously interesting features of the region I have tried to tell, and if I have failed, it is in part because their grandeur is too surpassing to be adequately treated by my pen.…

So my camps for another year are at an end. The old rifle has had its final cleaning and is put away, the knife is rusting in its sheath. The story of my summer is at an end, and as I have so often done before, I close the notebook and say good-bye.[30]

2

1886

Meanwhile, Back in New York

THE AUDUBON SOCIETY

Very slowly the public are awakening to see that the fashion of wearing the feathers and skins of birds is abominable. There is, we think, no doubt that when the facts about this fashion are known, it will be frowned down and will cease to exist. Legislation of itself can do little against this barbarous practice, but if public sentiment can be aroused against it, it will die a speedy death.

The *Forest and Stream* has been hammering away at this subject for some years, and the result of its blows is seen in the gradual change which has taken place in public sentiment since it began its work....The reform in America, as elsewhere, must be inaugurated by women, and if the subject is properly called to their notice, their tender hearts will be quick to respond....The women of America...can accomplish an incalculable amount of good....

Our beautiful birds give to many people a great deal of pleasure and add much to the delights of the country. These birds are slaughtered in vast numbers for gain....In a three months' trip a single taxidermist collected bird skins to the number of 11,018, which would perhaps represent a destruction of 15,000 birds. This same person states that he handles annually about 30,000 bird skins, almost all of which are used for millinery purposes. A single middleman who collected the spoils of the shooters in one small district, brought to the taxidermists in four months about 70,000 birds....

FOREST AND STREAM.

A WEEKLY JOURNAL OF THE ROD AND GUN.

TERMS, $4 A YEAR. 10 CTS. A COPY.
SIX MONTHS, $2.

NEW YORK, FEBRUARY 25, 1886.

VOL. XXVI. —No. 5.
Nos. 39 & 40 PARK ROW, NEW YORK.

Above: Forest and Stream masthead.
University of Arizona Archives.

Left: Fine Feathered Friends.
Audubon Society.

We propose the formation of an association for the protection of wild birds and their eggs, which shall be called the Audubon Society. Its membership is to be free to everyone who is willing to lend a helping hand in forwarding the objects for which it is formed. These objects shall be to prevent, so far as possible (1) the killing of any wild birds not used for food, (2) the destruction of nests or eggs of any wild bird, and (3) the wearing of feathers as ornaments or trimming for dress....

Those who desire to join the Audubon Society, established on the basis and for the purpose above set forth, should send their names at once to the Forest and Stream, 40 Park Row, New York.[31]

~The response to Grinnell article was overwhelming. Thousands joined and numerous influential people sent letters to Forest and Stream showing their support. The Honorable Oliver Wendell Holmes wrote to deplore "the waste of these beautiful, happy, innocent and useful lives on which we depend for a large share of our natural enjoyment."

The poet John Greenleaf Whittier wrote, "I heartily approve of the proposed Audubon Society. We are in a way to destroy both our forests and our birds. A Society for the preservation of the latter has long been needed."

And from Charles Dudley Warner: "A dead bird does not help the appearance of an ugly woman."[32]

The public began to respond immediately. Within only one year, the membership exceeded forty thousand. Using the resources of Forest and Stream Publishing Company, the Audubon Magazine was introduced in February 1887, distributed monthly and sent to subscribers for fifty cents per year. However, the free-membership society and magazine would only exist until January 1889 due to the expense and time required by the staff of Forest and Stream, which adversely affected the primary purpose of the publishing company~

"With the [January 1889] issue of The Audubon Magazine, Grinnell is obliged to throw in the towel....These tens of thousands of members....are too much for the limited Park Row staff."[33] When the organization folded, it boasted almost forty-nine thousand members.

"The Audubon Society movement [lives, and] its influence is still shown in the several societies here and there springing up first in one quarter and then in another and assuming the name of the original institution....By 1900 there will be Audubon societies in nineteen states....By the end of 1904, Grinnell in his chair at Forest & Stream, will be writing yet another installment of the Audubon saga. It is proposed....to incorporate a National Association of Audubon Societies whose membership shall cover the whole country."[34]

~The national committee of Audubon societies was organized at a meeting held in Washington, D.C., in 1902. The year 1905 saw the creation of the National Association of Audubon Societies for the Protection of Wild Birds and Animals, with George Bird Grinnell named a director. The national organization eventually numbered hundreds of independent society chapters.~

Vol. I.   February, 1887.   No. 1.

THE AUDUBON MAGAZINE

Published in the Interests of The

AUDUBON SOCIETY

for the

PROTECTION OF BIRDS

FOREST AND STREAM PUBLISHING COMPANY.
NEW YORK.

Annual Subscription, 50 Cts.   Single Copy, 6 Cts.

Audubon Magazine, February 1887. *Audubon Society.*

THEODORE ROOSEVELT

~In his book, Wilderness Warrior, *Douglas Brinkley describes the efforts of Theodore Roosevelt, the former New York State congressman, to write about his hunting trips in the Badlands of the Dakota Territory. In the fall of 1884, Roosevelt decided to write a book, so he organized his notes that he had made after hunting in the Badlands and the Bighorns. He, a conservationist at heart, decided to combine his views about natural history with his big-game hunting trips. The book was eventually written in his home in New York City. The final manuscript consisted of ninety-five thousand words and was completed in March 1885. He titled it* Hunting Trips of a Ranchman.

After it was published a few months later, impressive reviews began to be published. Among them, the New York Times *said that the book was clear-eyed and would seize "a leading position in the literature of the American sportsman." But one review, which was generally positive, stood out as being somewhat contrary. Published in* Forest and Stream *was an editorial by George Bird Grinnell, who placed his sights on Roosevelt and fired away.~*

Roosevelt has not become accustomed to all the various sights and sounds of the plains and the mountains, and for him all the difference which exists between the East and the West are still sharply defined....We are sorry to see that a number of hunting myths are given as fact, but it was after all scarcely to be expected that with the author's limited experience he could sift the wheat from the chaff and distinguish the true from the false.[35]

~Grinnell pointed out Roosevelt's failing in not describing the differences among various game animal species, including color variations, size and other details relating to zoology. Grinnell specifically mentioned the antelope (correctly called pronghorn) species found in Montana as being different from those found in the Canadian provinces. Grinnell admonished Roosevelt for being a first-impressionist as opposed to being more scientific with more detailed research under his belt before putting his facts, not his impressions, to print.

After reading the review, Roosevelt stormed into the offices of Forest and Stream *demanding a meeting. Always cordial, Grinnell agreed. To Roosevelt's surprise, Grinnell was easygoing and allowed a few hours to review the book page by page. This young editor—he was thirty-six—seemed to know more about bighorn sheep and white-tailed deer than he did. The conversation turned to conservation issues, specifically big-game protection. Their views on big-game protection were almost identical, and they bonded. Grinnell told Roosevelt about game destruction of several species in Montana for the hides only, which, so far as small game was concerned, had begun in the West only a few years*

Hunting Trips of a Ranchman cover.
Author photo.

before that. The buffalo herds were essentially gone. Straggling buffalo were occasionally killed for some years after this, but the last of the big herds had disappeared. Elk and deer herds had been drastically reduced in size.

Both men had ideas about an outdoor sportsmen's organization. Grinnell related his ideas about creating good sportsmanship among all hunters, outlining hunting guidelines to provide wildlife conservation, and fostering government legislation about the environment. Roosevelt concurred. The result of their conversation resulted the following year in the creation of the Boone & Crockett Club.~

In *Wilderness Warrior*, Douglas Brinkley asserts, "By the time Roosevelt left the headquarters of Forest and Stream no lingering animosity or grudge would spoil his new friendship with George Bird Grinnell, who fast became as close a friend as Henry Cabot Lodge. When it came to saving wildlife the two men were in sync....To Roosevelt, Grinnell [became] an American treasure whose likeness should have been cast in granite. Instead of being rivals, Roosevelt and Grinnell united in what would become a lifelong crusade to save the big game animals of the American West from extinction."[36]

RETURN TO THE ST. MARY'S LAKES—OR NOT!

Letter to Schultz, August 23, 1886:

My dear Mr. Schultz,

You cannot conceive what a disappointment it is for me to give up all hope of seeing you this autumn and in making another trip with you....I had always hoped…to make it possible for me to go with you deep into the mountains whose outskirts we explored last year. I shall never be satisfied until I find out what lies behind the peaks that [surround] St. Mary and get close to some of the glaciers [in] these mountains. Let us think of the trip as only postponed a year.[37]

BOONE AND CROCKETT CLUB

Douglas Brinkley's *Wilderness Warrior* notes,

In early December 1887 Theodore Roosevelt…would create a hunting club [based largely on Grinnell's ideas] *devoted to saving big game and its habitats. High-powered sportsmen like himself, banding together, had to lead a new wildlife protection movement. As his first step, Roosevelt asked George Bird Grinnell to be a co-founder of the Boone and Crockett Club. Grinnell had already successfully created the Audubon Society and was editor of the respected periodical* Forest and Stream, *so he knew how to rally public opinion....Roosevelt convened some of the best and brightest wildlife lovers and naturalists in the New York area to dine at his sister's Madison Avenue home.*

Although Grinnell disdained lobbying, he was good at it. Grinnell fully approved of the project, and his willingness to join forces with Roosevelt to promote the conservation of big game animals and their habitat boded well for the eventual success of the Boone and Crockett Club. Roosevelt and Grinnell had lured a who's who of other conservation-minded "American hunting riflemen." All of the original twelve members had to espouse the "fair chase" philosophy and believe in the sanctity of national parks. In early January 1888, the twelve founders of the Boone and Crockett Club had approved a prescient conservationist constitution at Pinnards Restaurant in Manhattan.[38]

~The constitution had a distinctly Grinnell flavor. The Boone and Crockett Club, Roosevelt's and Grinnell's longtime dream, came into existence. A year later Grinnell succinctly described the club in an editorial in Forest and Stream~

The objects of the club as announced in its constitution are these:

To promote manly sport with the rifle.

To promote travel and exploration in the wild and unknown or but partially-known portions of the country.

To work for the preservation of the large game of this country, and, so far as possible, to further legislation for that purpose and to assist in enforcing existing laws.

To promote inquiry into, and to report observations on the habits and natural history of the various wild animals.

To bring about among the members the interchange of opinions and ideas on hunting, travel and exploration, of the various kinds of hunting rifles, on the haunts of game animals, etc. The Boone and Crockett Club is composed of men of social standing, whose opinion is worth regarding and whose influence is widely felt in the best classes of society. This club discountenances the bloody methods of all game butchers and no man who is guilty of slaughtering game can expect consideration from its members. These members are not slow to express their views about the folly and the wrong of wanton butchery, and their opinions on sport are therefore spread among that very class which in the past has given most offense in

George Bird Grinnell, Boone and Crockett Club co-founder. *Boone and Crockett.*

this respect. That within the last year or two a considerable change of sentiment has been brought about among men who have heretofore been very destructive to game seems quite certain. Those who used to boast of their slaughter are now ashamed of it, and it is becoming a recognized fact that a man who wastefully destroys big game, whether for the market or only for the heads, has nothing of the true sportsman about him.[39]

3

1887

Exploring the Glacier

*Appekunny…will very likely go with us. He is a good fellow,
and while he is not much on the hunt, he is a great fellow to catch fish,
shoot birds and loaf about camp.*
—*Letter to Luther North, May 18, 1887*
(Grinnell describing his entourage for his autumn trip)

About a glowing camp-fire on the shores of the St. Mary Lakes are seated three persons.…H.G. Dulog (the Rhymer), [an anagram for George H. Gould, a good friend of Yo,] Appekunny, and Old Yo. Their camp is pitched in a little grove of aspens.…It is very quiet; even the soft lapping of the water on the pebbly beach.…is stilled tonight. At intervals the footfall of one of the horses is heard from the darkness without the circle of firelight, or the swishing sound of a picket rope dragged over the grass as one of [the horses] shifts his position. The men are silent. It is the magic hour after dinner, when, tired after a long day's march, their appetites satisfied, they are content to sit still and be lazy.…

Gould came from California over the Canadian Pacific Railroad. [He met Yo, as prearranged, on October 1 in Lethbridge, Alberta.] From the south came Appekunny, that [adopted] Piegan, traveling on horseback over the yellow prairie.…Yo had come furthest of all, from the Atlantic coast over the Canadian Pacific.…[T]he railroad journey had been delightful.

The travelers by rail had met Appekunny at Lethbridge, and there had left civilization for their camp on the lakes.…Five or six days' travel brought them to the lakes, and now that their goal is reached, they recline at ease

George H. Gould. *Yale University Manuscripts and Archives.*

about the fire, and this camp calls up memories of a hundred others ....The fire is burning low, and Appekunny, rising, throws two or three sticks upon it, and the loose bark of the dry aspen logs catches like tinder, burns up and makes a cheerful light, which rouses the others from their dreaming and the Rhymer tells a story of the Blackfeet Nation.

For a short space there was silence. Then more logs were piled on the fire, the horses were looked after and those most likely to wander tied up, and then all hands turned in.[40]

OCTOBER 10

If anyone had put his head into the tent of the Rock Climbers one morning early in October, he would have been surprised to see it all so quiet....In its sheltered position the tent was loaded with snow and the light within was dim, as if the dawn was just breaking. Motionless within their warm blankets the occupants were waiting for daylight, but as it did not come they began to stir, and at length from one end of a pile of blankets a hand was stretched forth, which fumbled about for a moment among the clothing which served for a pillow, and then drew forth a watch. Then came the cry: "Hullo, boys, it's eight o'clock....It must be snowing."

Five minutes later, all hands were astir, and the state of the weather was being discussed....Snowfall would have been an advantage had they been nearer their hunting ground, but, as it was, it meant mud and difficult pulling over the few remaining miles which lay between their present camp and the upper end of the lower lake.

All the morning the storm continued; but by noon the snow had ceased falling, and before long all hands had started out to see whether there was any prospect of finding game in the vicinity. [None was found.] Toward evening the animals were transferred to a wide flat across the creek where the grass was thick and sweet, and here picket pins were driven and the horses staked out.

OCTOBER 11

By the next morning the snow had almost disappeared. The tramp of the day before had made it evident to those who had followed the trail up the shore that, with their light team, it would be impracticable to haul the wagon to the head of the lake. But if power to move it could be supplied, the boat, which was cached in the brush at the outlet of the lower lake, was large enough to carry all their goods. Appekunny is stalwart and well able to tug the laboring oar, but the Rhymer is an invalid and Yo....is troubled with a certain chronic laziness.

Talking the matter over the night before, it had been decided that another man must be had, and it was whispered that the right one might be found at a whisky trader's camp at Pike Lake, about ten miles distant.[41] Schultz knew that his friend, J.B. "Jack" Monroe, was hunting in the Pike Lake area, so he sent [old Yo] off to find him.[42]

Letter to Jack Monroe, November 20, 1918

I have a keen memory of the way that Steve [a bootlegger-friend of Jack's] *dived into the brush when I appeared over the hill at Pike Lake* [above your camp] *and cached his whiskey. It was more than two months later that on the road to Lethbridge* [Alberta] *I met him* [walking] *on the road to America* [after spending time in] *a British jail* [after being caught by the Canadian mounties].

OCTOBER 12

It was high noon at the St. Mary Lakes when [Yo and Monroe] rode across the river, up the bank, and into the camp. Dinner was on the fire, and [the] ten-mile ride had given the new arrivals a good appetite....After the meal was over, preparations were made for a start up the lake. The wagon was hauled down into the brush on the shore and so carefully cached there that it was invisible unless one knew just where it was hidden....Then followed the transportation...of the possessions of the party, and for an hour there was hurrying back and forth between the beach and the camp. Gradually a pile of baggage of rather appalling dimensions arose by the side of the boat. At length it was all there, from the tent pins up to the grub box, and the work of stowing the boat began....Jack and Appekunny sprang in and took the oars, the boat was shoved off, and they started up the lake. Then the Rhymer and Yo went up the bank, gathered the horses, and put the saddles on them, jumping on their own to start along the trail....

You can easily fancy that the Rhymer and Yo enjoyed their ride up the lake....An occasional flash from the oars in the sun as they rose

Flattop and Singleshot Mountains. *Author photo.*

and fell told [the riders] that it was their craft....At last, the inlet flat was reached....[T]hen they turned north [and] passed Mad Bear Creek....In a few moments we were in sight of the white tent, which gleamed among the willow and alder bushes on the very shores of the lake.

It was an ideal camp. In front was unlimited water; behind, grass for a thousand horses; and at the right, wood enough to last half a dozen years.... From the water's edge, half a dozen steps from the tent door, the whole expanse of the lower lake was in view, while behind it across the grassy flat and hardly more than a rifle shot distant, rose the steeply sloping foothills, above which towered the bare gray rock walls of Flattop and old Singleshot....In due time the boat was unloaded, and the travelers were comfortably housed and felt themselves at home. "Well," said Jack as he entered the tent after changing the horses to fresh grass, "if we're going to start at daylight tomorrow, we've got to get the boat up the inlet tonight." "We may as well do it now," responded Yo. "It will take us till near sundown as it is. Come on, Appekunny."[43]

OCTOBER 13

They had determined to make a trip by water to the upper lake to try to get some goats. Yo urged this. So far, although they had been in camp here two or three days, nothing eatable larger than a chance duck or grouse had fallen before their rifles, and they were getting hungry for something more substantial in the way of fresh meat.

The Rhymer and Jack were going through thick pine timber on their way up Singleshot when they came on some very fresh bear sign. They followed the tracks which grew constantly more fresh, and at length they [smelled] the animal. They went forward as quickly as possible and yet with the utmost caution. Suddenly, 100 yds. below them and lying down under the upturned roots of a fallen tree, Jack saw the bear and whispered to Rhymer, "There he is." There was no time for investigation, (a single bound would take the black object out of sight) so the rifle jumped to the shoulder and spoke out, but the bear never moved. "Look at it through the glass," said the Rhymer in a hollow voice, for dreadful doubts began to force themselves upon him. Jack did so. The Rhymer had fired at a bear, but this particular bear, though pierced through and through by the hunter's deadly ball, turned out to be only an old black stump, and so was not brought into camp.

Grouse and ducks are capital eating and had been greatly enjoyed, as had also the great lake trout that had been lured out of the depths of the lake, but the men all felt that one thing more was needed to make camp thoroughly comfortable. That one thing was a piece of fat meat hanging upon the tree that stood close by the tent door. On the Upper Lake it was thought that they could surely get a goat or two, and it had been decided to try to secure one on the following day.

OCTOBER 14

Long before daylight next morning the camp was astir, and the first gray streaks were just appearing in the eastern sky when the four men, carrying only their rifles and the photographic camera, started for the boat....[They set out to] attempt the seven-mile row which must be accomplished to bring them to the ground on which they proposed to hunt.

Before the sun had risen they had pushed off from the shore....It was cold, and the ice which had formed in the boat during the night showed no signs of melting. At length the sun rose, flooding the scene with genial light and heat and raising the spirits of the shivering men. The row up the lake was beautiful. At length the boat passed through the narrows where the long steep ledge of rocks running down from Otu Komi almost reaches the mountains on the opposite side of the lake....Goat Mountain on the right (north) and Red Eagle on the left (south), though equally steep and stern, were yet utterly different in appearance....It had been arranged that Appekunny and Yo should hunt on Red Eagle, while the Rhymer and Jack should cross the lake and hunt in Monroe Basin, a locality famous for the numbers of goats which frequent its rough sides, and equally renowned for the difficulties of ascending those sides. The boat touched the shore, and two of the hunters disembarked. After setting up the camera and taking two or three views of the lake, they started to climb the mountainside. Their prospects for success did not seem good, for in cold and snowy weather the north slope of a mountain is not the place to look for game....

Meantime the boat had crossed the lake and landed in a little cove, where the Rhymer and Jack had left it, and made their way into a broad basin. The climbing was rough and steep, chiefly over hills of sliding shale. The two followed up the basin for several miles but saw no goats....At length, turning their steps toward the shore, they took to the oars, and by three o'clock were sitting about a fire that they had kindled on the beach where they had left

Upper St. Mary Lake. *Author photo.*

Upper St. Mary Lake Narrows. *Seward House Museum.*

Red Eagle Mountain. *National Park Service, West Glacier, Montana, Hileman photo.*

their comrades in the morning. They shouted in the hope of hurrying them, for there was a long row before them, and the sun was lowering toward the mountain tops. At length their calls were faintly replied to, and presently the others…came out of the timber and gladly drew near the fire.

Jack, who had been examining Goat Mountain with a glass, had detected a number of goats on it, and a careful inspection revealed eight or ten of these animals moving about and feeding over its sides….Here at last was something definite and positive, and the hopes of the hunters rose high. Presently all hands tumbled into the boat, and the return journey began. A bitter wind blew from the west and helped them on their way, but it was very cold. The row occupied but two hours, and by the time the landing was reached two or three of the party were so stiff with cold that they could hardly get out of the boat.[44]

OCTOBER 15

Started about 8 A.M. in large boat for a goat hunt on upper lake. It took us about 3 hours to get to our destination….The climbing on this mtn was exceedingly arduous and often difficult, and as we were on the N side of it, the ground was covered with snow and ice….[We spotted no game and eventually began our descent to the lake.] Reaching the shore at 5:15 we found our companions who had seen no game but had shot the head off a Franklin grouse. The row down the lake, although the wind was behind, seemed very long and slow, though it occupied only just over 2 hours….We were wet with perspiration and snow water, and the wind pierced our very marrow….On reaching the mouth of inlet I was so stiff with cold that I could barely get out of the boat to walk the remaining [shore] to camp.[45]

October 16

That morning by 8 o'clock all the horses were saddled, and soon after, the four men were loping as hard as they could go toward Goat Mountain…. Tying the horses in a little park surrounded by spruces…the men stepped out to the edge of the grove and looked the hillside over for goats. One at least was discovered immediately, lying in the shade in a crevice of the rock. He seemed but little larger than a pea, he was so far above them, but looking through the powerful glass one could see his horns and the shadow cast by his ears.

Their plans were soon laid. Yo and Appekunny were to keep on straight up the mountain, to go around the animal and try to approach it from above, while the Rhymer and Jack, taking a lower course, should endeavor to reach it from below….Then after a pipe had been smoked, the men rose to their feet, took up their rifles, and set their faces to the task before them.

The climb for those who had the lower course was rough and hard. They moved along the face of the mountain….always working a little higher up on the mountain and nearer the game. Appekunny and Yo, who kept on up the shoulder of the mountain, found their climbing not difficult, though very steep. With many pauses for breath, they kept at it, and after an hour and a half found themselves on the lower edge of a steep slope…. From here they could see the goat still lying in the crevice of the rock and now not more than 500 yds distant. It was cold here, and in the bitter wind the breath froze, so that moustache and beard were ornamented with great icicles. [T]he goat did not find it so, for he had chosen a spot well out of the sun, and there, just below a mass of snow and close by a frozen rivulet, he was lying in the shade trying to keep cool.

The upper part of the slope…was bare of trees and in plain sight of the goat, and in order to get above him it was necessary either to cross this or to go back and around.…They started crawling on hands and knees and keeping as close to the ground as possible. The open spot was about 50 yds across, and they had passed over half of this distance when the goat slowly rose to his feet. Without moving a muscle the two men lay there and watched it.…For five minutes it stood there, then slowly turned and walked back to the seemingly vertical wall behind it, raised itself on its hind legs, and raised itself awkwardly, drawing up its hind legs and giving himself a push with them which sent it up to a little jutting point of rock where there was room for all four feet.…The whole movement was as slow and clumsy as could be imagined and yet wonderfully strong and effective. The animal did not seem in the least frightened; there was no indication in his movements that he had been alarmed. He went up the cliff with the utmost deliberation, stopping every now and then to take a bite of some tempting bit of vegetation, and often waiting for a moment or two to think something over.

At length he disappeared over the top of the cliff.…[Appekunny and Yo] started on up the mountain to reach its crest. It was noon before this was done.…Having reached a point half a mile above where the goat had last been seen, the men left the crest of the ridge and advanced along the mountainside.…Appekunny and Yo passed along the mountainside about 50 yds apart.…They had started for the cliffs, when suddenly a white spot came into view on one of the nearest cliffs. On examining it with a glass it was seen to be a goat lying down on a shelf of the cliff just above the slide rock.

Carefully they stalked it, passing cautiously from tree to tree, until at length a point of rocks concealed the animal from view. Then hurrying forward they peered carefully around the last point of rocks.…The animal must be beyond one of two points just before them. It was not seen beyond the first of these, but on rounding the second, there lay the goat on his little shelf just as he had been when first discovered.

Yo was anxious to get the animal. It was the first goat at which he had ever had a fair shot and the camp needed meat.…[H]e took a careful and rather long aim, and as the shot rang out and was thrown back by the cliffs above and tossed about from crag to crag the goat sprang to its feet. As it rushed across the narrow shelf on which it had been lying, it was seen that its left foreleg was swinging helplessly, evidently broken high up.…[A]s it had been lying a little quartering toward the sun, a ball that had broken its shoulder must have passed through heart or lungs. The goat ran to the edge of the shelf as if about to leap off, but the plunge of 60 ft. straight

Mountain goat on a mountainside ledge. *Author photo.*

down was too much for it. It turned and ran back toward the crevice, down which it had come and reared against the rocks as if to try to ascend. As it did so, Appekunny fired a shot which struck the rocks in front of it, and it again ran back to the edge of the shelf. Just as it reached it, its knees gave way, and it pitched forward, whirling over and over through the air, struck a ledge and bounded out again, rolled over and over down the slide rock into a narrow, smooth water course guttered out of the slate. In this channel, it slipped, slid, and rolled over and over, an inert mass, down the mountainside and out of sight.

"Hurrah," shouted Appekunny. "You've got him, sure enough, and you ought to, for you took a long enough aim."…

Yo followed the animal down the mountainside, springing from rock to rock.…Down where the goat had tumbled into the ravine the rocks were plentifully besmeared with blood; and 50 or 60 yds further down, the animal lay dead. It was a female two-year-old.…

It took some little time to drag the carcass onto a convenient shelf for working on it and to get it in shape for transportation down the mountain.…

The chances of their getting into camp that night were small. Hurrying down the mountainside they struck the trail, Appekunny in the lead with the head, hide and shoulders of the game on his back, while Yo followed with the hams and saddles. They traveled as fast as possible....By this time it was getting dusk and had begun to rain.

The horses were a mile above the trail on the mountainside...so presently Yo turned off to get them....By the time he reached the horses he found that Appekunny had also come for them and was starting down the hill. It was now quite dark and raining, and as he picked his way slowly down the hill, dragging after him his unwilling horse, he heard a wail like that of a lost soul rise out of the darkness below him.

"Look out for the trail," was the cry. "I can't find the trail; I've lost the trail." And the echoes took up the sounds, and rocks and pines called back *trail, tra-i-l, -ail, -ail,* 'til the air was full of the dismal murmurs. Presently the men met down in the timber, about where the trail should be, and after a little they found it...then lost it, found it again and so went on for half a mile very slowly and unsatisfactorily.

At last Appekunny said, "Let's camp. We can't find the trail, and if we could I don't propose to risk my neck going down on those rocks in the dark."...

A few yards back was a little open park where there was some grass for the horses, and here they unsaddled, tied the horses, and built a fire. They had no food nor water, but the night was mild and the rain had ceased falling so that there was every prospect that they would be fairly comfortable. The fire was built near two large spruces, and it took but a short time to find a slender pole which was run across the lower branches of these trees about six feet from the ground. Over this pole the saddle blankets were hung, forming a lean-to, which reflected back the heat from the fire and which was warm and comfortable while the fire lasted. It took only about an hour for this to burn down, and then one or other of the men would get cold, rise to mend the fire and smoke and get warm, and then would end up again and take a little more sleep. All night long the geese could be heard talking on the lake not far from them, and other flocks coming in and announcing their arrival in trumpet tones. The sky had cleared, and the night was warm; there was plenty of wood and the men were comfortable and contented.

October 17

At last daylight came. The horses were saddled, the trail found at once, and an hour and a half later two very hungry men were in camp eating breakfast faster than the two others could cook it for them.[46]

October 18–19

The weather was cold and threatening, and ominous clouds hung low over the mountains of the upper lake....The next day the wind was blowing furiously....On the upper lake and on Singleshot it was snowing hard with a good prospect of a general storm....By noon all the mountains were shrouded in storm clouds, and soon it began to rain furiously at the level of the lake....As the shades of early twilight began to fall, the occupants turned to and cooked their simple meal, and soon after rolled themselves up in their blankets to sleep quietly in spite of the howling gale.

October 20

During the night the storm passed, and the next morning it was bright and pleasant....Everything was wet, however, and it was necessary to dry ropes and blankets before a start could be made. When this had been done, two days' bread, bacon, coffee, and sugar were laid out, the beds made up into side packs, and by noon Split-tongue [the mule] was packed, the two horses saddled, and the men moved out for Red Eagle Lake leaving the camp to take care of itself....

At length they crossed to the west side of the creek, passed through some open timber into a little park where there was a recent Kootenay camp.... On the upper side of this was a little group of trees, the chief of which was a mighty spruce with widely spreading branches, and under this the horses were halted, saddles and packs taken off, and camp made. The horses and mule were picketed in the little prairie, the beds spread down together under the spruce, a lot of wood collected, and a fire started. There was still an hour or two of daylight left, and the men went down to the creek to try to catch some fish....Appekunny, who had baited a hook with a piece of bacon and thrown it into the deepest part of the pool, gave a wild yell and rushed away from the shore followed by a fine 2 lb. trout, which did not stop until he was

Red Eagle Creek and Lake. *Minnesota Historical Society, Louis Hill photo.*

safely flapping among the rounded pebbles on the bar from which they were fishing....Appekunny presently caught another on his hand line. Then Yo, putting a bit of bacon on one of his flies, caught a fine fellow that made the supple rod bend and the line hum through the water in fine style. Then, as it was becoming dusk, they took their way to camp, where trout, bread, and coffee furnished them a substantial and delicious meal. The night was cold, and it was raining a little.

October 21

It was still raining a little the next morning, when shortly after sunrise the two men were on the shores of the lake. They at once espied two goats.... After waiting an hour, first one and then the other lay down. Then having taken careful note of all their surroundings, the hunters started up the mountain side....At length, they reached the ledge on which the animals were supposed to be lying, but after working along it nearly to the end of the mountain without seeing anything, it was decided that they must be lower down. The men therefore went back and clambered down two ledges.... Presently they passed around a point of rocks, and Yo saw a small goat lying down on a point of rocks about 75 yds distant. It was broadside to us and had one foreleg doubled up under it, the other being stretched out before it. Its eyes were closed, and it seemed to be asleep....

Without a moment's delay Yo fired, and the goat sprang to its feet and made a step forward, which took it out of sight behind a great rock, and as it disappeared Appekuny called out, "Look, below you at the other." Turning his eyes to the left, Yo saw standing on the edge of a grassy spot and close to the timber another and larger goat. Again the report rang out, and as the ball struck it, the animal leaped high in the air so that it almost seemed as it if were going to turn a back somersault....It came down on its feet, however, and with a single bound disappeared in the brush below it. "Good," said Appekunny, "you've got that one, anyhow. He's going downhill."

"I never saw any animal jump in that way," answered Yo, "except on receiving a fatal wound."

The tired men started down the hill to look for the other goat....On reaching the level on which the goat had stood when shot at, the men separated....A shout from Appekunny told that he had struck the trail. All along the track the blood was scattered on the ground as if it had been thrown down by teacupfuls. As they went down the hill side by side there was a continuous thick blood trail which assured them that the game could not have gone far....So they followed the trail straight down the slope...for about 100 yds. There at the bottom of a broken precipice 50 or 60 ft. in height, they saw the goat, dead. It was a female, two years old, and like the previous capture had never bred.

The animal was in very fine condition, and they saved the whole of it.... At length they were ready to start, and Appekunny as usual led the way with the hide, head, and shoulders, while Yo followed with the hams and saddles and a bag containing the heart, liver, and ten or fifteen pounds of tallow. The loads were heavy enough to make them glad to rest at frequent intervals, but the way down was not difficult for they followed the side of a deep gorge....

By this time Yo's load had become very heavy, and he made but slow time through the down timber and over the rocky undulations of the valley....That night the hungry hunters feasted on fat meat. The bread allowance was very short, however, and the next morning's meal would consist of meat and coffee.

After supper the meat was hung up in a tree, and a lot of wood was gathered. It was raining a little, and the wind moaned in the trees with an ominous sound. It looked as if it were "fixing for a storm," but it was hoped that they might have one more day of fair weather so as to reach their comfortable main camp before the storm set in."[47]

OCTOBER 22

...Appekunny and Yo rested well on their last night at Red Eagle Lake, but when [Yo] put his face out from beneath the piece of canvas....he received a chilling baptism which thoroughly awakened him. Three or four inches of snow lay on the canvas, and a mass of this told its own unpleasant story...and the sooner they got away the better it would be for them. While breakfast was being prepared, the horses were looked for....Fortunately they were all found in a sheltered corner of the park and were soon brought close to camp and tied there. Then ropes, blankets and saddles were resurrected from beneath their snowy covering and brought close to the fire to thaw out and dry....

Breakfast over, the packs were made up, and Split-tongue saddled. The side packs were put on and the swings tied, but as the center pack...was being lifted on, the little mule dodged, twisted and in a moment...was bucking and galloping across the little park, pursued by the invectives of the careless packers....The men followed and caught Split-tongue standing under a tree a couple of hundred yards away. The saddle had turned so that one of the side packs was under her belly and the other was on top of her back. Returning to the fire, the men repacked successfully, but...the pack cover was stiff with ice and snow, and the lash rope was frozen....

At length a start was made, and the little train moved off across the snow-covered park....With feet wet, gloves frozen and bodies chilled, the men were uncomfortable enough and anxious to push on as rapidly as possible.... They rounded the timber near Mad Bear Creek and saw the familiar spot, and presently the white tent showed through the falling snow. The dogs had run ahead and by their barking had notified the Rhymer and Jack of the arrival. In a moment more, two shadowy figures had stepped out of the tent and were seen through the flying snow, watching their approach. The thick smoke which curled up from the fire indicated that cooking was going on, and Yo called back to Appekunny the word "Dinner" and the stiffened faces of the two gradually changed their set expressions and slowly creased themselves into responsive grins....

Darkness was closing over the lake when they reached the camp, but half an hour later they were enjoying their delicious supper. They laughed at the hardships of the day's march and pronounced their excursion an unqualified success.[48]

They had plenty of wood and the greater part of three fat goats hung upon a tree within 8 ft. of the tent door.

OCTOBER 23–24

Last night this meat caused a little excitement in camp. It was perhaps two o'clock on a bright moonlight night, when Yo…heard a noise as of something falling, followed immediately by the sound of galloping quite near the tent.…The dogs at once set up a tremendous barking, and the sound of the retreating footsteps stopped so quickly that it was evident that no horse had made it.…Jack got up and stepped out of the tent. He called out, "Something has carried off a ham of meat," then an instant later, "Why, I see the darned thing there in the brush!" Jack reached into the tent for his gun, and both men cheered on the dogs who could be plainly seen against the white snow in the bushes dancing around a dark object sitting there.… Encouraged by cries of "Sick him, Keno; go for him, Babbette," the dogs mustered up pluck enough to rush in upon the creature, but they did not stay there long.…Meantime the creature had once more turned his attention to the meat. "Well," said Jack, "I guess he calculates he'll drive us out of camp, but we'll see first if we can't get that meat back." He then fired four shots at the animal, which calmly went on with its meal until the fourth shot had been fired, when it again sprang into the air and bounded off into the deeper shadows of the brush. Jack stepped out to where the animal had been, picked up the ham, brought it back and hung it up in the tree.…The next morning before breakfast Jack went out from where the meat had been and returned with a little tuft of hair, gray mixed with rufous, which had been knocked off by the ball and evidently belonged to a lynx or a wildcat.… After breakfast Jack and Yo took their rifles and started out on the animal's track to see where it led. It was readily followed…and about thirty steps from where it had left the meat was a bed where it had lain for some time, and in this bed was a drop or two of blood.…They followed the tracks very carefully.…When they had gone nearly a hundred yards, the tracks swerved suddenly to the right.…Jack made a motion with is hand and stopped, and Yo saw the animal not twenty yards away. It was lying in the sun at the foot of a great spruce tree, and only its hips were visible from behind the tree. Jack motioned to his companion to shoot....At the report the animal gave a spring and stretched itself out on the snow in the death agony. It proved to be a Canada lynx of the largest size....They carried the carcass back to camp and skinned it.

OCTOBER 25

At length there came a day when the cold broke....One morning it was observed that the wind had changed from cold to warm, and presently the snow began to melt. One after another little brown patches appeared on the flat behind the tent, and tufts of grass began to show their heads above it. For two days the chinook continued—a soft warm wind which played havoc with the work that winter had done. The ice disappeared from the lake, and the south hillsides became bare. The next day at noon [I] went up to inlet and shot a snow goose.

OCTOBER 26

And now came a mournful event—a parting. The Rhymer's time was up, and one afternoon he and Jack packed a mule, and after hearty hand-clasps rode away, the Rhymer to return over the Canadian Pacific Railway to his Western home, while Jack, after escorting him to the settlements, was to return to the camp.[49]
~After the Rhymer had departed, several days were spent quietly about camp and on the mountains. A little game was killed, a few photographs taken and, most remarkable of all, a new arrival welcomed to the lake.~

OCTOBER 28

Remained in camp all day fixing up skins. About 10 o'c saw coming up this trail on opposite end of lake a mounted man and a fine horse team. The glass showed that it was a soldier outfit. Our rifle signal was not answered, and they rode away.

October 29

Lt. Beacomb [*sic*] of 3rd Infantry, Ft. Shaw, called this A.M., and after breakfast we rode about halfway up to the point that runs into the upper lake and took a couple of pictures of Singleshot. Then came back and lunched with Beacom....We have determined to start for Swift Current tomorrow A.M. This P.M. was spent in packing our stuff into the boat.... The night was a beautiful one, and the moon, almost full, was about 3 hours high when I started at 7 P.M. For the first hour I had an abominable time, for the horses and mules did into want to go....The clear white moon light lighted up the prairie and the mountains with the light almost of day....The air was still. Windmaker slept, and his servants were at rest....I crossed the river and drove the horses to the appointed place, turning them loose at 9:30. I then built a fire on the beach as a guide to the boat which arrived ½ hour later.[50]

The blankets were thrown on shore, the boats hauled up and secured, Yo's horse was picketed securely near camp, and presently the men spread their beds and laid down to rest under the cold moon.[51]

October 30

It took some time to pack and cache all our stuff, and it was between one and two o'c when we started with 3 pack animals for Swift Current....Mr. Beacom started with us up the creek....The lieutenant has kindly allowed me to use a shot gun carried by his party....[52]

The sun was low in the west when they reached the first of the Swift Current lakes, in the lower end of which great numbers of Canada geese were resting and feeding. These as the train came in sight began to call to each other in tones of alarm, and at length took flight....Before a satisfactory camping ground could be found it was quite dark, but it took only a few moments to unpack, get a fire started, and [have] supper cooking. The camp was a couple of miles below the ordinarily-used ground near the fifth Swift Current lake, and at this season of the year... it was likely that grass [for the horses] would be scarce anywhere further up the stream.[53]

OCTOBER 31

The next morning the camp was astir before daylight, and preparations were made to start off on an exploring trip to see if a way might be found which would lead the traveler near to the ice which lies at the head of the great gorge....Breakfast eaten, the four men started, following the trail which led up through the much-used camp ground under the frowning face of an unnamed mountain, and by the shores of Fifth Lake, until they had passed above its head. Then turning off to the left, they plunged into the forest to try to find a trail toward the ice. Sometimes the branches of the pines were so low that they threatened to sweep the riders out of their saddles, or the slender trees stood so close together that there was barely room for a naked horse to pass between them. The men's knees were savagely ground between the trunks and the saddles....At length the timber became a little more open and the willows disappeared; then an old Indian trail...was met and followed for a while....Through openings in the timber one could look up a narrow valley toward the ice. A little later the trail passed into a natural avenue perhaps thirty feet wide, and led the travelers directly toward the vertical face of the stupendous mountain which stands between these two branches of Swift Current. This high narrow peak rises straight up for thousands of feet into a slender pinnacle or spire, and which shuts out every other point of the landscape....

At length they reached the head of the [sixth] lake, and descended to the creek by a rough series of steps, down which it sometimes seemed as if the horses must fall headlong on those who were leading them. From the gravel bars where the stream entered the lake a fine view of the glacier was had, and it looked as it was not more than four or five miles distant.

After taking one or two photographs from the head of the lake, they mounted their horses again and rode up the stream bed toward the ice. Half a mile brought them to the edge of a snow slide, the path of an enormous avalanche which years ago had rushed down the mountain side, cutting through the timber a swathe several hundred yards in width. From this point was had a view of the ice far better than anything that had yet been seen, and it was determined that on the following day a heroic effort should be made to reach it. Then the photographers began to set up their instruments....[P]resently they packed up their cameras, and mounting, started for camp.

"Stupendous" mountain. *Author's collection.*

Grinnell Glacier, 1887. *Beacom photo in lobby of Many Glacier Hotel.*

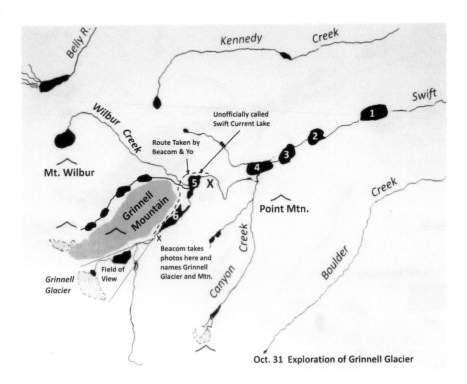

Oct. 31 Exploration of Grinnell Glacier

At the head of the lake the party divided, Jack and Appekunny following down the southern shore, which seemed to promise the shortest if not the easiest way to camp, while Lieutenant B. and Yo went back as they had come, stopping by the way to take one or two pictures.[54]

Diary Entry, John H. Beacom, Oct–Nov 1887:

I had the good fortune to fall in with Mr. Grinnell, Natural History Editor of Forest and Stream, and I enjoyed his hospitality and society for three days. I accompanied him up Swift Current and we photographed the glacier at the head of that stream, which in honor of him I called "Grinnell Glacier."[55]

Bird wrote in his journal: "[I] protested and he may not carry out his intention."[56]

~In "Early History of Glacier National Park, Montana," 1919, Madison Grant states: "At the same time, Mount Grinnell received [its name] from Lieut. Beacom." Yo later learned that Lieutenant Beacom was a member of the U.S. Geological Survey. Jack and his partner found a used Kootenay trail, which took them home very easily and quickly, but the others were longer on the way and did not reach camp until dusk.~

NOVEMBER 1

Early the next morning the necessary provisions for a four or five days' trip were put on the two little mules, and a fresh start was made for the glacier. Lieutenant B. who was unable to climb owing to an old hurt and who felt obliged to return to his camp at the lakes, said goodbye, and the three men plunged into the forest on the trail by which Jack and Appekunny had reached camp the night before. The way was not everything that could be desired. It was exceedingly narrow, sometimes scarcely wide enough for a man to ride along, and, as the mules were not very experienced pack animals, they had a good deal of trouble in getting through. In order to better distribute the load the blankets had been packed separately, instead of being rolled as usual in protecting canvas, and before they had gone very far, Yo, who brought up the rear of the procession, began to notice fragments of bedding dangling from the branches and tree trunks which he passed. He recognized the rags as belonging to the quilt in which he was accustomed to wrap himself each night. He shed a silent tear to its memory. The trail, in fact, was so narrow that it tore the packs to pieces. Progress was so very slow that it was the middle of the afternoon before they reached the head of [sixth] lake. Above this there was not known to be any feed for the horses, and it was therefore thought best to camp here. The animals were unpacked, led across the head of the lake, and turned loose on the grassy mountainside. The men spent the rest of the day looking over the mountains with their glasses.[57]

NOVEMBER 2

The moon had almost reached the tops of the western mountains when the Rock Climbers rose from their bed of boughs and made ready for a long day's work. Deep silence lay over the narrow valley where they, perhaps the first of all white men, had slept.... [T]he fire began to crackle, and the familiar sounds of camp were heard. Breakfast was soon eaten, the beds rolled up, and each man's load made ready. Appekunny put the camera on his back; Jack took the shotgun and a few shells; Yo buckled on his cartridge belt and took his rifle. With Jack in the lead, the three strode silently away through the forest on the east side of the stream....A mile and a half above the camp they came to a wide, rapid mountain stream which enters the valley from the southwest, through a broad canyon. [It reminded Yo of a horizontal cataract, so that night he made a note in his field journal to name it Cataract Creek.] They waded through this and soon came to an open meadow dotted here and there with little spruces. Beyond this they could see that there was no timber, and in a few moments they stood on the shore of a beautiful glacial lake.

Started off for Grinnell's Lake, as we have named the one which flows into 5th Swift Current Lake.[58] (Ed: Grinnell Lake actually flows into a sixth lake, which was named Lake Josephine in 1911. In his 1885 journal, GBG concluded that sixth lake was, in fact, an arm of fifth lake. In his 1887 journal, he mistakenly referred to the sixth lake as the fifth.)

It was circular in form, perhaps a mile across, and on all sides except that where they stood, was walled-in by vertical precipices of tremendous height. Immediately above it was the glacier from which flowed the dark green waters of the lake. On every side the walls dropped straight down into the deep waters, and along their smooth sides it seemed impossible to pass. At the head of the lake there is a narrow fringe of willows, then an open meadow of small extent, broken on its eastern side by a low, rocky, pine-crowned promontory, which juts out from the foot of a frowning peak, [which we named Monroe's Peak.][59] [The tall mountain behind, Yo later named Mount Gould.] Behind the little meadow rises squarely a thousand

Monroe's Peak and Mount Gould. *U.S. Geological Survey photo, author annotations.*

Right: Bird drinking water from Cataract Creek. *University of Montana Archives*.

Below: Grinnell Lake—looking north toward Grinnell Mountain. *Author photo*.

feet of black precipice, divided into two nearly equal halves by the white waving line of foam which rushes out from beneath the glacier and plunges downward, dashing itself to spray in its fall. On the right, as they faced the ice, another still higher mountain rises abruptly in a series of rocky ledges one above another, to a great height, and then terminates in a knife edge of naked pinnacled rock, cold, hard, and forbidding. Beyond is the tremendous mass of the glacial ice.

Here…they made their way around the lake. Sometimes they crept along almost on hands and knees over the steep and slippery rocks…stepping cautiously from rock to rock, balancing themselves with extreme care lest a misstep should send them sliding down the slope and into the cold waters below.…The cliff they wished to ascend was very steep, yet the climbing did not seem hard.…They marched steadily on, stopping now and then for a moment's breath, and at length reached the ledge. Along this they walked until they reached the very bed of the falls, and here began the serious work of the day.…Slowly and carefully they climbed upward, often crossing the stream from one side to the other clinging with tenacious grip to each little spruce twig, thrusting their fingers into the crevices in the rock and fitting their feet on every knob or projecting splinter or roughness that would aid them. Sometimes holding on with elbows, knees, calves, yes even with their chins.…So, inch by inch and foot by foot they made their way upward.… About two-thirds the way to the top of the precipice they came out on a shelf, perhaps one hundred feet wide, which was almost covered with high-heaped debris brought down by the glacier from above…composed of boulders and gravel of all sizes, from masses as large as a small house to grains no larger than a pin's head.

The white, quivering falls are very fine. They rush down the cliff, often by vertical plunges a hundred feet or more in height or down sharp inclines.…Everywhere there is spray, and often clinging to the vertical walls of the cliff are great masses of white ice, the arrested current of some little spring or offshoot of the stream. Keeping to the right over this great mass of morainal drift they gradually ascended…until they reached the level of the lower border of the glacier. It lies in a basin two miles wide by three or more deep, and consists of two principal masses, the lower of these covering a great extent of ground and running up into the little ravines and gorges of the mountains on either side. The upper mass seemed smaller than the one below. It rests on a ledge which runs far back among the peaks, and in its slow motion is constantly falling over the cliff and uniting with the lower mass.

Grinnell Glacier Waterfalls. *Yale University Manuscripts and Archives.*

It is impossible to do more than guess at the thickness of this ice, but from the edge of the lower mass to its comb the men estimated the vertical distance at about 700 ft. The thickness of the upper mass is perhaps 300 ft....[60] [Because of the slope of the glacier on the mountain shelf] the two together occupy 1500 to 2000 feet vertically on the mountain side.[61] (Ed: In 1888 field journal, using scientific instruments, the measurement was recorded at 1,850 feet.)

....After reaching the borders of the glacier the men followed it around to the right, for it was impossible to walk up the steep glare ice which lay between them and the comb of the lower mass....At one point Appekunny carelessly tried to shorten the way by climbing up over some old snow which was quite steep. Before he had gone very far...he slipped, recovered himself, stood for a moment, took another step and his feet flew out from under him. He began to slide down the steep snowdrift....The men had no inclination to smile. Happily nothing serious resulted. After going about a hundred yards at a high rate of speed, Appekunny ran into some snow that was soft and stopped. He made his way cautiously back to the edge of the rocks and

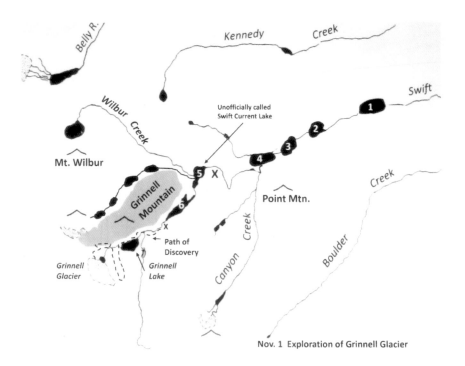

Nov. 1 Exploration of Grinnell Glacier

took the safe but longer road followed by his companions. Since it was past noon, the men sat down under the lee of one of the ridges and with good appetite ate their lunch of bread and cheese, and smoked.[62]

The men had come quite near to the rocky point about which some tracks passed...when Appekunny, who was further to the left, suddenly stopped and called out: "Si-YA! Look at that ram!" His eyes were fixed on the point, but neither Yo nor Jack could see from their point of view anything that warranted excitement. Quickly stepping to Appekunny's side there came into view as fine a bighorn as it is often given one to see. Standing there on the white snow....with his head thrown back as he gazed more in curiosity than alarm at the three strange creatures that approached him, he was a picture of unconscious grace, beauty and wildness. At Appekunny's first word Yo had loaded his rifle, and as the ram appeared he said, "How far, Jack?" "About 200 [yards]" was the reply, and Yo, dropping on one knee, fired. The rifle was aimed at the neck just below the throat to allow for the drop of the ball. The smoke hung for an instant, and when the rifle was lowered the animal had disappeared. "Did any one see where the ball struck?" asked the shooter. "Not I" said Appekunny. "Nor I" said Jack.

They hurried up the slope, and before they had gone far a cheer came from Jack who was in the lead. "Hurrah, Yo. Blood on the snow, and lots of it." Yes, sure enough, they could see even at that distance that the pure white mantle of snow was splashed with great blotches of red blood. The ram was evidently hard hit. The men followed at their best pace, Jack and Appekunny running around the point while Yo allowed his impetuosity to get the better of his judgment, and clambered directly up the rocky ledge toward the place where the dogs were evidently holding the animal.... Two hundred yards ahead of him were his companions, looking along the mountainside beyond them, and as they saw the belated rifleman approaching, they sat down to wait for him.

"Have you seen anything of him?" asked Yo as he came up. "No" replied Jack, "but the dogs followed the trail as far as that point of rocks over there, and he evidently turned down the hill."

"He is our meat, I guess then," said Yo, "Suppose you take my rifle, Jack, and follow the trail and get the sheep. Appekunny and I will go back and see some more of the ice. When we get through we will come down and join you."

The rifle and half a dozen cartridges having been given him, [Jack] started along the trail and was soon seen working his way diagonally down the mountain over the rough precipices. Yo and Appekunny now turned back to the glacier....Through the side canyon the two men walked down over this tributary of the ice river to the comb of the main lower ice, and out nearly to the middle of the glacier. Before them...it lay spread out far and wide, but behind them the cliff and the steeply inclined mass of ice cut off the view. They could see far down the valley of Swift Current into the flat at the foot of the lower St. Mary's Lake where their camp had been....A little to the south of west...lay a vast mass of sky-blue ice, reminding them of a time when the thickness of the glacier upon which they then stood was so much greater than at present that it covered even the towering peaks and walls which now form the summits of these mountains. Venturing close to the cliff over which the upper ice is slowly flowing to join the lower mass, the two men looked down into a seemingly bottomless abyss where the ice had melted next to the rock, but they did not care to venture too close to this on the hard, slippery snow, for, without ropes, the outlook for one who might fall into this crevice would be rather dismal.

Meantime Jack had followed the bloody trail along the mountainside.... [I]t would be seen that the quarry had stumbled and fallen and slid along on its side over the snow, leaving a broad smear of crimson on its otherwise unsullied whiteness. The little dog, Babbette, had accompanied him, and after [Jack] had gone more than a mile he rounded a point of rock and came upon the sheep which was lying down with lowered head, and in front of it stood Babbette, licking its nose in very friendly fashion....The animal rose to its feet, staggered a few steps, walked out of [a snowbank] to a cliff over which it fell, and when Jack got to it...it was lying in the snow, dead....

Yo and Appekunny presently saw Jack standing by a fire in a little valley below them. The fire was a pretty good sign that he had some meat, and the two men began to feel hungry....Yo hailed Jack, and he came up the stoop to meet them. A short distance away...lay the animal. He was indeed a beauty. Five years old, his horns were not very large but were perfectly symmetrical and unbroken....The work of preparing him for transportation to camp was undertaken at once....The animal was so heavy that...it was estimated that partially dressed he would weigh from 250 to 300 lbs. Jack...took off the forelegs and shoulder blades and came along with those....

They made their way down the mountain without much difficulty....

We had gone but a short distance when we passed on the lower side of a great snow drift in a gulley. [W]ater had tunneled under it below, so that a heavy roof stretched across the ravine. I entered and was astonished at its beauty. It was eight to ten feet from floor to roof and perhaps thirty ft wide

Ice cave. *Seward House Museum.*

and sixty to seventy long.…The roof seemed not to be more than eight in. or a foot thick and admitted the light quite freely. It was beautiful sky-blue ice and had melted from the bottom so as to form a curious pattern of squares.…It was lovely.[63]

They made good time through the timber, and at length reaching the camp, they threw down their loads with a sigh of relief.…When the fire was blazing and the fat sheep meat sputtering in the pan and the coffee pot steaming on the warm ashes, they talked over the incidents of the day. All agreed that a wonderful amount of enjoyment and interest had been compressed into the hours that had elapsed since their start that morning. Yo summarized the day in his journal: "A most important day, for we reached the glacier, discovered a new lake, a most beautiful falls, [a] true moraine at the foot of a glacier, and I killed a superb ram."[64]

NOVEMBER 3

…The day after the ascent of the glacier, Jack and Appekunny…caught two horses and went up stream to climb the mountain and bring down the [rest of the] meat of the sheep.…Reaching the base of the precipice, they climbed it and reached the place where the sheep lay. They then…brought it to the summit of the cliff, and lowering it down from shelf to shelf by means of ropes which they had provided [and] got it to the lake shore. Then [they] carried it on their backs to the horses, which packed it into camp. It was a long and hard day's work, and when they reached camp that night they were thoroughly exhausted.

Yo, whose note book was somewhat behindhand, and who wished to bring it up to date, determined to remain in camp. [He wrote for several hours.] During this time he was able to sketch the view from the campsite location below the glacier which they ascended.[65]

~On this sketch he identified the geological features he discovered that he had mentally affixed names to. Yo named a tall mountain to the southwest of the campsite Mount Gould and the point in front Monroe's Peak. He honored Appekunny by naming the northeast flank of Grinnell Mountain "Appekunny Mountain."[66] The glacier lay to the west of Grinnell Lake, and on his sketch Yo indicated the path of the waterfall from it to Grinnell Lake below. The "creek in woods" running from the bottom of the sketch is Cataract Creek. The large mountain in the lower right part of the sketch remained unnamed until 1891, when Yo named it Mount Allen. Yo finally accepted the names suggested by

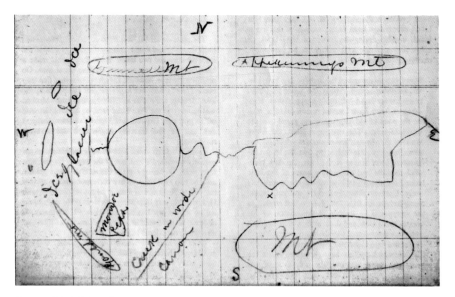

George Bird Grinnell sketch of Grinnell Basin. *University of Montana Archives, 1887 Journal.*

Lieutenant B., Grinnell Glacier and Grinnell Mountain, and in years to come he referred to the glacier as "my glacier." Grinnell Basin, suggested by Beacom, was absent from the sketch, and the sixth lake GBG saw from his campsite would be named Lake Josephine in 1911.~

NOVEMBER 4

...The morning after the meat had been brought down from the mountain, two of the men crossed the lake after the horses, while the third put things in shape for packing up and returning to the St. Mary's lakes. The men were gone a long time, and when they made their appearance they had only six horses. One was missing....

The loads were more than twice as heavy going out as they had been coming in, and so had to be newly arranged. The hams, saddles and ribs of the sheep made a good load for one of the mules; the remainder of the meat and the head, with the camera and cook outfit, went on the other. The bedding was all put on the pinto....The men put their blankets on the pinto...and started...for the valley of the main Swift Current....A red object was seen on the other side, which was at once recognized as the missing horse....Crossing the creek Appekunny went to him on foot, while the others kept on through the down timber, and presently they reached the trail. At their old camp they stopped, gathered up the articles left there, repacked, and then kept on down the valley.

Night overtook them before they reached the lake, but next morning… they were back at their old camp at the foot of [Lower St. Mary's Lake]…. So one by one the difficulties of the journey were overcome. The weather had again turned bitter cold and again all the standing water was frozen solid. The men put on all their extra clothing but often walked for warmth leading their horses. Sometimes when passing close to a timbered point they would halt for a while, build a fire, and thaw out.[67]

NOVEMBER 5

Up before light, but as the horses had not been picketed last night, they could not be found for two or three hours. Just as we were packing the second animal, Sgt. Dubbs rode into camp on a mule with a note from Lt. Beacom, saying he was going to move out and that he sent a man for the shotgun.…I then took a quarter of sheep and rode over to the soldier camp across the St. Mary's where I found them all ready to move. Had a talk with Beacom, telling him about the ice in G's Basin and giving him a sketch of the valley and my ideas as to the glacier. He kindly offered us any grub of which we were short, and I got some sugar, bacon, and coffee from him. Returning to our camp I got some tobacco which I have been without for 24 hours, and the men went off to the cache while I remained here, writing up notes.…Tomorrow we expect to make harnesses and next day shall try to pull out for Cut Bank.[68]

NOVEMBER 6–15

~The group mosied their way toward Cut Bank, hunting and fishing and eating sheep in various hunters' recipes.~

NOVEMBER 16

...A few days before reaching Cut Bank...the weather showed no sign of improving. At last one day came a very heavy fall of snow, and it turned bitter cold. It was time to start.

Early next morning the wagon was packed....All day long [we] traveled, and just about sunset, [we] came to the South Fork of Milk River, two or three miles above Sam Bird's ranch, which [we] reached after dark....The cabin was 16 ft. square and was pretty well occupied that night, there being already three men, a woman and a baby in it, besides uncounted dogs, cats and chickens. The travelers were welcomed, and they slept there that night....[We] Rock Climbers spread [our] beds on the floor, the cats crept in with them, and the hens cached themselves under the table. It was all as comfortable as you please....

It had been cold enough before, but during the night the temperature had fallen still further, and in the morning when [we] were out gathering the horses it was found that the river had frozen so hard that the horses could walk across it without breaking through. This was the end of the Rock Climbers' trip. Jack had his reasons for going no further and left [us] here, while Yo and Appekunny, with little besides the former's personal belongings in the wagon, started back to Lethbridge to get to the Canadian Pacific Railroad....

The next morning the animals had been brought in and hitched up, and Appekunny and Yo drove away. The distance from the crossing to Lethbridge...and by going by way of Brown's and George Houk's, the distance was less than fifty miles....Eventually, after a few days driving the wagon they drove up to Houk's cabin. The next day they reached Lethbridge and parted. The Rock Climbers would climb no more.[69]

4

1888

Honoring Piegan Friends

~Bird decided on this trip that he would focus more on collecting data toward making a map of this area. Weather instrumentation and a sextant were among his belongings. He also decided to record information about the birds east of the Continental Divide. So he left New York armed not only with a fly rod but also with the necessary items needed to accomplish these new things.~

On the bed nearest the door as you enter the lodge [tipi] sits Jack, the Outlaw [Jack Monroe], busy with awl, needles and waxed thread, patching his worn-out shoes....Next to him sat Appekunny, crosslegged like a tailor, and busied in putting a patch on that part of his trousers which is most used when one is at church, or in the saddle, or at dinner. Yo is the next man, sitting pipe in mouth on his bed and doing nothing, and next to him comes the [Little] Chief [Captain Luther North], that ancient Pawnee warrior who has been Yo's companion in so many scenes of happiness and of hardship....Next to them, and so across the lodge from Appekunny, is the stalwart form of the Rhymer [George Gould], who with his moccasined feet stretched out toward the fire, and a dainty cigarette held between his lips, is perhaps composing a poem, but more probably is dropping off to sleep. And last of all, near the woodpile, his bronzed face bent toward the fire, and his coal-black hair hanging down toward his hands, is [Tail-Feathers] Coming In Sight Over The Hill [known as Brocky], a noted warrior and hunter of the Pegunny.[70]

OCTOBER 2–3

Weather mild and pleasant, a good west breeze before sunrise, later calm. Thermometer 37°, wet bulb 34, humidity 71%, bar. 25.05 in. All at 6:00 a.m. Lute & Gould went to set line and caught a big trout, guessed at 3 ½ to 4 lbs. Wind fell about noon. Packed 3 animals after noon and started for Swift Current, up which we went 8 or 9 miles. At camp after supper, head of Second Lake. Bar. 24.55 in. Weather mild. Wednesday was calm & pleasant at 6:30. Bar 24.50 in. Ice of Grinnell's Glacier in sight. Packed and got started at 8:40. A breeze sprung up from the west. Reached camp about 10:00. Put up tepee, and about noon with Lute started to try to climb the mt. Got up 2150 feet from falls and lake and then gave out & returned to camp. At current bar 24.60 in., therm 60°, wet bulb 57, hum 86%.

OCTOBER 4–6

Calm & pleasant but hazy. At 8 o.c. bar 24.60 in., therm 32°, hum 79%. Lute & Brocky started for the Red basin on N. Fork Swift Current. Followed Kootenay trail to torrent which is now dry, and left horses 825 ft. above camp. Climbed up through the basin to a height of 7050 ft. above camp. No sign of sheep to amount to anything as there is no water. Bar. 23.80 in. Wind fresh changing later to calm. Bearings taken from lower end of lake in the opening above falls:

Highest point of Gould's Mt. S 10° W.	Gould's distant about 8 m.
Highest point of Monroe Peak S 20° W.	Monroe's Peak distant about 7 mi.
Highest point of Appekunny's Mt. S 34° W.	Appekunnys distant about 1 ½ mi.
Highest point of Mt. Wilbur W 28° S.	Mt. Wilbur distant about 15 mi.

Falls are East 50° S, distant 150 yds. Reached camp at 5 o.c. and found that Gould, Jack & Brocky have gone on to glacier lakes, leaving Appekunny to go on with us. We got off as soon as possible but night overtook us at the little prairie and we camped there; no supper. Bar 24.57. At camp just before leaving, therm 59°. w.b. 56, hum 57%. After many difficulties in timber, reached camp at upper glacial lake in sight of glacier.[71]

OCTOBER 7

The lodge was pitched at the foot of the Upper Glacial Lake. To the northeast ran the narrow trough through which Glacier Creek flows to join the main Swift Current, but on every other side rose mountains, steep, ragged, snow-patched: the homes of the white goat, the bighorn and the white-tailed ptarmigan. The vertical rock falls above these snow and ice fields, and the deep narrow clefts in the rock, are favorite feeding grounds for the white goat. Here, up a steep long slide, the Rhymer had stalked a great male that, unconscious of his approach, continued to graze on the tender plants until he felt the bullet's fatal sting, and then sturdily making his way up the rocks, exposing himself to other shots which finally brought him rolling down the steep incline.

The Chief today saw his first goat. It was browsing on a cliff far above the valley....Having crept along the narrow ledges until he was within range, the Chief shot it, wounding it so severely that it was unable to climb. It had strength enough, however, to walk along a ledge and on behind a point of rocks where it lay down. The hunter followed it; he fired a shot hoping to make it move to a point where he could kill it. At the report it rose to its feet,

White goat. *Wikimedia.*

walked around another point of rocks and again lay down....The goat lay there looking at him, but neither [Chief's] shouts, nor the stones which he threw at it, had the effect of making it get up. It was impossible to approach it where it lay, and the Chief shot it through the heart. As the ball struck it, it gave a convulsive spring, fell forward into the ravine, rolled down that to a snow bank, over which it slid until it reached some slide rock, where it again began to roll over and over, and at last shot out over a waterfall and disappeared, not to be seen until sometime later when it was found on a ledge behind the waterfall several hundred feet below. The chief declared that it made him quite weak to watch the animal's fall and to think that if he should slip, [it] would probably be over the same ground....

Yo was anxious to make the ascent of the mountain, and it was determined to carry up a little food and some blankets and to camp at the highest point where wood for cooking could be had....Yo and Appekunny had started early in the day, carrying rifle and camera, and were to be followed somewhat later by Jack and Brocky, who should bring up food and bedding....Yo and Appekunny began the ascent of the mountain on the north side of the valley, climbing laboriously up the steep slope until they reached the ledges.... When the ledges were reached the climbers made their way from one to another through narrow crevices torn out from the rock by the torrents

Grinnell Falls from Grinnell Lake.
Yale University Manuscripts and Archives,
Reel 46, George Bird Grinnell photo.

which in spring rush down from the melting snows.... [T]hey had been gone five hours before they reached the lateral moraine on the north side of the glacier. Here they sat down to look over the ice while they eat their lunch.

At the time of their previous visit to this spot the glacier had appeared much more extensive than it did now. It was now melting rapidly, broken by crevasses and scored with streams of swift-flowing clear water. The torrents which poured forth from beneath the blue ice were white as milk, for they carried with them a fine powder, the ground up rock of which the mountain is composed. Along the lateral moraine, on the north side of the ice, were freshly turned up rocks and earth, which showed that the glacier was now moving.

Descending from their perch upon the moraine, the men moved onto the ice. Its surface showed no new snow, and it was soft and everywhere melting. Down the steep slope of the ice hurried a dozen swift torrents, which had worn for themselves deep channels in which they whirled, until at last they plunged into some deep crevasse and with hollow roarings disappeared from view. The blue icefield was dotted far and near with fragments of rock, great and small, with mud heaps and with great quantities of other debris which had fallen down on the ice from the cliffs above. The ice was slippery beneath the feet of the men who now ventured on it, and as its surface was sharply inclined they were obliged to move very carefully. The deep crevasses, with which [the glacier] was everywhere seamed, were alarming, for they seemed bottomless. If a man should fall into one of them he would never be seen again. They had with them a coil of light rope taken from one of the pack saddles, and with this they tied themselves together, only one man approaching the crevasses at a time, the other standing at some little distance so as to hold his companion in case the latter should slip.

The glacier was vocal with the sound of running water. The musical tinkle of the tiny rivulet, the deep bass roar of the dashing torrent, the hiss of rushing water....fell upon the ear, and up through the holes and crevasses in the ice came strange hollow murmurs, growlings and roarings, while the whole ice mass seems to shake and quiver from the concussion of the masses of water that are rushing along beneath it. Many of the crevasses were too deep to be measured by the 100 ft. fishing line which Yo carried in his pocket; others seemed to be not real crevasses, but mere fissures in the ice 25 or 30 ft. deep and partially filled with clear water, through which the blue ice of the bottom could be plainly seen.

The sloping face of the ice was not easy to walk on, and if it had not been for the occasional stones which now and then gave a secure foothold, it would have been impossible to move about on it at all. Yo, who was very anxious

Crevasses in Grinnell Glacier. *National Park Service, Elrod photo.*

to reach the crest of the mountain, started to climb up the west arm, which showed a gradual slope from the moraine up almost to the high saddle from which the west arm of the glacier starts....He started up the slope, walking carefully, and supporting himself by means of the stock of his rifle, which at every step he dug into the soft ice. Appekunny followed, but in a short time concluded that the rocks were "good enough for him," and made his way to the edge of the ice and sprang to the ground. It was not long before Yo wished that he had done the same thing. The ice grew more and more steep and more and more slippery, and the footing less secure. The fragments of rock lying on the ice became less frequent, and it was each moment more difficult to plant his feet in the ice. He tried to make his way to the rocks at the side of the glacier, but a wide chasm yawned between the ice and *terra firma*—a chasm too wide to be jumped. Below him was the steep ice slope a mile in length and ending in a series of crevasses. Above was the steep, smooth face of the glacier. A slip of the foot might result in a fall, and the man, if he fell, would go sliding down the ice with no hope of stopping before the crevasses were reached. If engulfed in one of these his case would be hopeless. Yet this particular mode of going out of the world did not seem especially alarming, for it was certain that if he started to slide down this slope he would be dead before he reached the crevasses, since the rock fragments that dotted the ice would have stripped all the flesh from his bones before he had reached the end of the slope. Only his skeleton would fall into the crevasse.

At all events there was but one thing to do; he must continue to climb. It was a slow, toilsome and very delicate journey, the last half mile of this climb, but at its end Yo found himself within 75 yds of the end of the west arm. Here further progress was barred by a wide crevasse, beyond which the ice sloped so sharply that no living thing could have climbed it. Making his way to the edge of the ice, he at length found a place where a shoulder of rock projected out from the cliffs to within 3 or 4 ft. of the ice, and by a careful spring he crossed the gap and kept on his way up toward the saddle.…It took but a few moments to reach the saddle, from which point Yo could see far to the west.… At length, turning his face from this pleasant scene, he took his way with hasty steps down over the rocks toward the glacier's foot and before very long, joined his companion. The sun had set, and it was growing dark when they climbed the great moraine near the glacier's foot and hurried down toward the timber. They could see the flicker of the firelight where Jack and Brocky had evidently made camp. Before long they were warming themselves by the grateful blaze.

Though their food was scanty that night, and though their resting place was but a few paces from everlasting ice and snow, they slept well and rose refreshed. After breakfast Appekunny and Brocky started down to camp with the beds, while Jack and Yo crossed the moraine at the foot of the glacier and clambered to the saddle between Monroe's Peak and Gould Mountain. The clouds were flying over the mountain, and the wind was blowing hard, presaging a storm.…From the side of Monroe's Peak can be seen the whole valley of Cataract Creek, and from their lofty perch they looked down on the spot where a day or two before they had seen the white goats then so far above them. To have pushed on further over these heights would have been pleasant, but the fast-falling rain forced them to hurry toward camp. They did so, but the rain continued, and when that afternoon they reached the lodge they were thoroughly soaked.[72]

Our lodge is an ordinary, conical one, such as is used by the Northern Indians, 12 ft in diameter and as many in height. At the top is the smoke hole, through which, smoking up through the cloud of gray vapor that rises from the fire in the center, one can see dimly a star or two. The fire burns brightly, and every now and then someone puts on it a stick or two of the finely split open wood, partly for the warmth, partly for the light and partly to make a high blaze which will keep up a good draught and carry the smoke well upward. At about the height of a man's head the smoke spreads out and fills the upper part of the lodge, but then no one ever stands up in a lodge. On lines stretched about the lodge poles, five or six feet from the ground, are various articles of wearing apparel, placed there to dry. There are socks and shirts, boots and shoes, trousers and a coat. The walls of the dwelling are brownish black, darkest above, where the smoke has done its work, and shading into paler below, where only dirt and actual wear and tear have stained them. Down on the ground floor you could see, if you had this scene to look back on as I have, to the left of the door our cooking utensils and our sacks of flour, bacon, and sugar, then the beds, stretched close to the walls, around nearly to the door again, where are the woodpile and the water bucket. The beds are not very wide and there is abundant space for the fire in the middle of the floor. This is our home; here we spend our time, laughing at the storms of rain, sleet and snow, which daily burst upon us from the mountains, and lulled to rest by the roar of the warring elements.[73]

OCTOBER 8–10

I found that the lower end of ice was 350 feet below camp so that the whole vertical extent of glacier is 1850 feet. The greatest width is about 3 miles and its depth perhaps 1½ to 2 miles. It rained all of the afternoon and much of the night and the lodge leaks a little, not being properly stretched, as we have poles too large and not enough of them—only 8. On the whole we are comfortable. Next day, everything wet, but rain has stopped. We shall start as soon as day. Put out things to dry. The others went fishing and caught some whitefish. At 7:15 next day Bar 24.70 in, meaning height of this camp approximately 400 ft. above foot of lower lake. Have had good sharptail [grouse] shooting on prairie, and now want blue grouse. Brocky shot grouse.

OCTOBER 11

During the night it rained slightly and toward morning quite hard. At breakfast the weather was gloomy and threatening with occasional rain squalls. Took weather readings often during the day. Getting ready to move [to the St. Mary's Lakes]. Gould and Jack started about 2 p.m. in the boat with a sail and the wind being favorable east of north. They were soon far up the lake. We packed the wagon and followed. The weather was lovely, and the mountains beautiful. The pines so green, the aspens so golden and the lake so blue. We went along very well and just before dusk reached camp. Soon Jack & Gould who had been there since 4 o'c came in with four splendid trout weighing from 1½ to 4 lbs, and we had a delicious supper.[74]

October 12

Today it was clear and warmer. A Chinook had begun to blow, and on the lower level the snow was disappearing. The outfit of the camp was gathered up, and a great fire built, about which were spread out to dry blankets, ropes, saddles and other property. By mid-day the animals had been gathered and tied up, and the loads were being put on the horses. An hour or two before sundown camp was made at the old spot at the head of the Upper Lake.

Meat was needed in camp. The goat meat was not highly esteemed and even Tail-Feathers-Coming-In-Sight-Over-The-Hill did not care for it. He expressed the general sentiment when…he remarked, shaking his head doubtfully, "Well, it *can* be eaten." It is true that we had had plenty of trout and grouse; we had not been brought down to eating bacon; still we wanted some "real meat," some sheep or deer or moose. So two of the old men declared that they would go hunting on the morrow.

Long before daylight next morning the Chief and Yo were stirring, for they purposed to clamber up on Singleshot Mountain to see if they could not find the little band of mountain sheep which were known to frequent the basin in which Mad Bear Creek rises.

It was just gray dawn when, the horses having been brought in and saddled and breakfast having been cooked, they mounted and rode off up the flat.…The two horsemen had not been on Singleshot that season, but when they had nearly reached the mouth of the inlet by the Upper Lake they turned up the hill and struck into the trail, which through the aspens was easily followed.…Clambering higher and higher, the men kept on until at length they came to the level bench upon which.…the last timber grows. Here the men halted, unsaddled, and picketed their horses so that they could rest and feed during the hour which their riders would spend on the heights above. The last act preparatory to moving on the heights before them was to sit down and smoke—the Chief rolling a cigarette, while Yo whittled some tobacco from his plug and filled his pipe.

When the last fragrance of the tobacco had been wafted along the mountain side and the ashes had grown cold, the men rose, and taking up their rifles, faced the steep ascent. A climb up a clay bank 200 ft. high brought them to the piled up rocks over which sheep trails led along the mountainside. Before they had gone 200 yds they saw the fresh tracks of three sheep which had been made that morning, but it was impossible to follow them over the rocks. The men pushed on until they were close beneath the wall rock and then followed a trail which led up into the basin between Singleshot and Flat Top. As they approached the crest of each little ridge their steps became slower and more cautious, their heads turned this way and that, and their eyes rolled as they scanned each foot of the country.

This morning the Chief was in the lead, and his keen eye swept the mountain side before and below him for an hour or more as the two walked slowly along under the frowning "reefs." At length the ringing sound of a rolling rock was heard below them, and at the noise both men stood still as statues and watched the rocks whence the noise had come. For five or ten minutes they stood thus....As they slowly went on, Yo saw the Chief throw up his rifle and fire a quick shot. An instant later the backs of two animals were seen above a ridge of rock two hundred yards below them....Yo at once pitched his rifle to his shoulder and fired at the narrow line of hair which was visible, but he heard the ball strike a rock and then go singing off across the valley. The back disappeared at once, but the hunters knew that the game would try to run around them and to climb the mountains; so both men hurried forward to cut them off....Slipping, stumbling, and half falling the men ran ahead as best they could. Yo, who was the lighter weight of the two, was somewhat in advance. Suddenly he saw appear over a ridge before him the head and shoulders of a ewe, and beside her the smaller figure of a lamb. There was no time to waste, as the animals would be out of sight in a single bound. Balancing himself on the moving rocks Yo fired at the ewe's shoulder. The report of the rifle was followed by a dull sound that indicated that the ball had hit the sheep. Yo called back, "I think I hit her, Chief. I heard the ball strike." "Good," was the response, "Follow her up and see where she is going."

Moving onto the ridge on which the animal had stood when the shot was fired, Yo looked over it and saw, lying down on a rock 30 yds beyond, the ewe, evidently hard hit, while by her stood the lamb. From the mother's actions it was evident that she had received a mortal wound and would soon die. The Chief crept down the mountain side to within range of the animals and fired at the lamb, but it did not fall at once. The two sheep then got up and turning back walked along the slide rock below the men, disappearing behind a great rock which the hunters could cover from their position. It was evident that the two animals needed only to be left alone, and so the hunters sat down and smoked....[T]hey again took up their rifles and began the descent of the hill. Presently they reached a point from which they could see the sheep. The lamb was lying dead, while the ewe...was evidently in the last agonies. In a moment she stretched out her legs, gave a few convulsive kicks, and began to roll over and over down the hill, falling at least a quarter of a mile before she stopped against a great stone.

Now followed the unpleasing task of preparing the meat for transportation and packing it out to the horses...[when] one of the heavily-laden men fell among the rocks, receiving a strain from which he has not yet recovered. At length the meat had all been carried out over the rocks and to the top of the steep bank, below which stood the horses. Down this bank it was rolled, and then came the packing it on the horse which was to carry it to camp. Neither one of the horses would pack meat, yet one of them had to. The men chose the Chief's mount as the one least likely to prove obstinate. Three times they tried to put the load on the horse, and three times it threw itself backward. Finally they blinded the horse and lashed the load on firmly, then removing the blind let it buck. It made desperate efforts to free itself, but the load stayed with it; finally it made up its mind to carry it. Starting on foot down the steep hill, they made good progress.[75]

Yo and the Chief were both...lame and sore from the exertions of the day, for each of them had packed on his back a heavy load of meat along the rough mountainside, now over smooth, sliding shale, or again over great rocks where the footing was unstable, and steps had to be now long and now short. As they sat there on this night, side by side, the silence was broken by a speech from the Chief, who turned to Yo and said, "Old Man, did you mind my laughing at you today when you fell and the sheep fell on you? I did not mean to, but you looked so funny when you disappeared in that crack with the sheep on top of you that I couldn't help it. Besides, I felt sure from the character of the remarks you made that you were not much hurt."

"I thought when I plunged into that hole and that sheep came down on top of me that I was broken in two," said Yo, "but I got nothing worse than a few bruises."[76]

October 13–16

Rained last night and the mtn tops are white with snow. Sore and stiff all over from back of neck down to soles of feet....In afternoon got boat up to mouth of inlet and fished, but it was too cold and windy. Skinned weasel. Next day still blowing and is cold. North & Gould will go to Point of Rock & boys follow with boat. Brocky caught mink. Started about 10, reached camp at 12. On Monday at old camp. Froze hard during night and a little snow. Left camp at 9 to look for sheep. Lute and I went high up above slide rock and Gould went down. After going a short distance Lute came on a yearling ram in a gulch 20 yards off and shot at him missing. I shot too. He went about 70 yds and stopped, facing us and Lute shot again. He went 50 yds farther, stopped again & I shot. [H]e disappeared behind some rocks. When I returned from hunting, I found camp moved to lake. Tuesday with Lute to try [Rose] Basin for sheep. Took the horses as far as lower ledge. Thence on foot around basin and over Otu Komi. Made fire at a height of 2450 feet above camp and then climbed to summit. Mt. pretty flat on top and almost bare of vegetation—nothing but slate and shale rock. On top saw four ptarmigan, one still speckled with brown on back of neck. They cock the tail up like a rooster. They cackle like a hen. Three of them had dug holes in the snow drifts and were lying in them for shelter from the fierce wind that was blowing. The barometer on top the highest point recorded 21.575 in., or 9025 ft. B. 24.65 in. Otu Komi is thus about 3800 ft. above the lake. Saw pine squirrel in basin, snowshoe rabbit in timber. Appekunny killed a gray ruffed grouse. [S]aw 2 goats on Red Eagle and 4 sheep on Singleshot from camp.

October 17

More or less rain and wind last night. This morning raining. Therm 39°. Rained all the morning. Many flocks flying south, most of them stopped by wind blowing down the lake and turned off east. We named peaks on southeast side of lake. The first as you go up the lake is Red Eagle, then Four Bears, then Little Chief, then Almost-A-Dog, all on SE side of lake." [Also named Citadel Mountain.][77]
~Red Eagle Mountain had previously been named by Schultz's wife, Natahki, when they were on a camping trip on St. Mary's Lake early in 1885. Schultz shared this story:~

The previous winter was a terrible one. We were actually snowed in. My uncle, old Red Eagle, had some pounds of tobacco in his sacred elk-tongue pipe bundle. My little son became sick, and his mother got Red Eagle to pray for his recovery—hours-long ceremonial prayers and songs....And the boy got well, owing, all said, to the Sun priest's prayers. Schultz had received a new boat, and in the spring he and his wife, Natahki, had been camping in the timber at the foot of Upper St. Mary Lake. When we were on the shore or out in our boat, my wife would often point to the first mountain on the east side of the lake and remark that she thought it the most imposing of them all, rising so steeply and to such great height, right up from the water....So now I shall name that mountain that I like best of all. It is "Red Eagle Mountain." Later during our trip she said: "That little lake, it will be Red Eagle Lake, and its outlet, Red Eagle Creek."[78]

~Bird made a note of the names in his journal after Schultz told his story.

"Four Bears Mountain" was named for Four Bears, who was a chief in the Mandan tribe and was the grandfather of Joseph Kipp. Later, topographers renamed the mountain in the Mandan dialect, Mahtotopah.

Red Eagle Mountain. *National Park Service, West Glacier, Montana, Hileman photo.*

Four Bears and Little Chief Mountains. *Author photo.*

Almost-A-Dog Mountain. *National Park Service, West Glacier, Montana.*

Mount Siyeh. *Flickr user dvs, CC 2.0.*

"Little Chief Mountain" refers to Captain Luther North, who was a company commander under his brother Major Frank North, who commanded an army battalion of one hundred Pawnee scouts. The scouts were employed by the army to provide protection for the Union Pacific Railroad. Lute was "Little Chief." (Frank was "Chief.") Bird first met Luther in 1872 on a Pawnee buffalo hunt. In 1874, he was Bird's naturalist assistant on the General Custer reconnaissance to the Black Hills.

Almost-A-Dog Mountain was named to honor a good friend of Bird's who was one of only a handful of survivors of the Baker Massacre on January 23, 1870. Also, during the winter of starvation, 1883–34, Almost-A-Dog kept count of his fellow tribesmen who perished by cutting notches on a stick—555 notches.[79]

Bird named Mount Siyeh (sah-YEE), a prominent peak to the northwest, to honor a Blackfoot friend, Siyeh (Mad Wolf). Siyeh in Blackfoot means "mad." So Siyeh Mountain—and later Creek, Glacier and Pass—came into existence.~

Siyeh Creek. *Author photo.*

The wind began to blow hard, and a long line of mist ran swiftly up the lake on the wings of a howling gale. As it reached us we found it was snow, and for six or eight hours it snowed furiously. The first blast of the wind threw down our lodge, and before long the ground was white with snow. Many flocks passed over—some of them early in the day, evidently meeting adverse currents of wind and being turned off their route. Geese flying all night. At no time very cold. Then at 4 o.c., 37°.[80]

October 18

Therm at sunrise 20°. It cleared during the night and the morning was beautiful, clear and windless. Breakfast by candlelight. Everything snow-covered, and the early light gave lovely effects on the snow-clad hills. Gould & Jack started for Goat Mt, and Lute & I for south point of Singleshot. Gould saw a goat far up, but it moved off and he got off no shot. Lute & I got into a most infernal tangle of down timber and brush as that it took us nearly 3 hours to ascend 1500 ft. Every tree & bush was covered with snow and we were plentifully sprinkled and wet. Built fire and warmed up, then went on. I saw no sign and after wading and wallowing till between then & 4 o.c. made my way toward camp which we reached at 6 p.m. Schultz reports therm 27° at midday. Strong west wind from noon.

October 19–22

[Made daily weather measurements to aid in mapping the area.] Clear, warm, strong west wind. A chinook seemed to be blowing. Laid about camp all day until one o'c. Then went to outlet. Jack and Appekunny going in boat, the rest packing part of stuff on mules. [Next day] went up on Singleshot with Lute through heavy & deep snow. Very cold wind. Saw nothing but 2 ruffed grouse and a falcon. Lute goes tomorrow. Wrote Mother. [Next day] Lute has gone. Started about noon and travelled by Red Eagle trail over which the South Piegans had followed earlier in the day. Left this trail six or eight miles from camp and bore to the south up the mtn and through timber. Camped in a little grassy meadow with willows and alders where there is feed enough for the horses for one day. Put up lodge and am comfortable. Heavy wind during night. [Monday] a little snow last night and this a.m. It is snowing in the mtns. After breakfast started for Kootenay Mt which we reached after three hour's hard climbing making some rather bad breaks in attempts to reach the saddle and getting up on the hill east of it. Saw tracks of moose, elk, sheep, bobcat, lynx, fox, wolverine, porcupine and many other small mammals. At last reached the saddle and found tracks made today but saw no sheep. It soon came on to snow and blow hard, obscuring the view, so after following along the mt side for half a mile or so we went down and into the timber and so home. My back which has been troubling me more or less for two or three days is tonight so bad that I can hardly move. I am convinced that I strained myself when I carried the sheep on a pole with Lute. Gould kindly did all the work, and I sat and watched him. Saw snowshoe rabbits.

October 23–25

Rained pretty hard all last night, and continues today. We are likely to spend the day today in camp on account of weather. Still raining heavily but we are not discouraged. At 8:30 p.m. changed to snow and it got colder with some wind. Next morning about 18 inches of snow. Weather mild, a little below freezing. Went out for 5 hours to look for moose sign but saw no tracks except those of a bobcat and a squirrel. Saw hudsonian titmice in numbers. Returning about 3 o'c. A quiet day. I began [to add onto the 1885 sketch map] what I recalled about the Swift Current Valley and east side of lower St. Mary's Lake. I will add mtns, lakes, and glaciers later. Forest beautiful in its covering of snow, but without signs of life. Early on Thursday it began to snow very hard and it was determined to move down to the main camp as the snow is too deep to hunt. Gould starts out for walk and I remain in camp to dry ropes and blankets. During his absence Red Bonnet & another North Piegan came to the lodge and warmed up. They were hunting on their way back from Red Eagle and had come upon our lodge. I gave them some coffee and bread and we talked. After a while they left. About two o'c we got started for camp in a blinding snow storm from the west. Reached camp about 4:30. The Indians had gone down just before us and had broken out the trail. But for that, we would have been an hour longer on our way. At camp found Almost-A-Boy who dined after us, and later Red Bonnet came and they told us Blackfeet names for game animals.

OCTOBER 26

During the night it snowed about two inches very light, but at daylight it was clear. Partially cloudy at sunrise and later on bright. Jack went out to look for horses with shot gun and brought back tree sparrows, two of which I skinned. After lunch went out myself and saw sharptailed grouse, swans, magpie, and plenty of ducks with some Canada geese. In the morning took two views [photos] of Piegan camp.

OCTOBER 27

Cloudy & threatening, but later clear. Snowing in the mts. Therm at sunrise 18°. Wind from the west. Indians got 4 sheep on Flattop and 4 on west front Singleshot. Wind blows heavily at noon and it is snowing in the mts. Weather cloudy, windy from west and threatening. At 2:30 or 3, furious winds from west which continued till after dark with some snow and rain. Walked down to lake and saw many gulls on sandbars. Killed one which proved to be Bonaparte's. Saw flocks of Bohemnian waxwing on Mad Bear Creek—a large one. Visited cache with Jack who put out some poison and saw tracks of lynx, wolverine & coyote. We saw about 12 ptarmigan on top of Otu Komi digging holes in snow to escape wind. At dark chinooking. Snow going fast.

OCTOBER 28

Rained during the night and this a.m. Most of the snow on the flat is gone. Raining a little and the mts hung with clouds. Hauled stuff to head of lower lake, raised cache & started boat down. Appekunny drove team and I [drove the] horses. We left camp at 11:30. Arriving at river found party from McLeod, 5 men and a halfbreed woman. Saw what I am quite sure were Barrow's golden eyes together with many geese and bluebills, some greebs & Canada geese.

OCTOBER 29–NOVEMBER 6

As we drove ourselves toward the railroad in Lethbridge, Alberta, we encountered rain, wind, and cold weather. We hunted along the Milk River as we advanced, shooting only sharptails [grouse] and a few ducks. No game was found. On Oct 31, Gould & Schultz got some very poor and short lodge poles with which we put up lodge. A little further up, the valley is covered with 8 inches of snow. On Nov 1, it snowed and blew during the night, and the lodge, owing to poor poles, came near blowing down, so that before light Jack & Appekunny got up and went to the timber and got 4 good ones. Took down lodge & put at up again. It still snows and blows.[81]

~In one week, they parted ways. Gould rode the CPRR to Santa Barbara, and Bird returned to his office in New York. Appekunny remained in Montana and returned to his family. They hoped to meet again the following year.~

5

1889

Goat Expedition in British Columbia

I have been the chief actor in a bloody tragedy, and like other guilty persons, I have an excuse for any dark deed....In some ways the occurrence was rather remarkable. Two or three years ago the directors of a great museum...applied to me for a series of properly prepared skins of [the mountain goat], from which to set up a mounted group of white goats. I had been informed that what were especially desired were a monster male, two females and two young ones—in short, a family. I had made vigorous efforts to supply these desiderate, and besides my own hunting, had employed men who live the year round in a goat country and who frequently hunt the animals, to look out for and secure the desired specimens. Through the efforts of one of these men the large male had been procured, but the kids were still wanting. I was becoming discouraged.

In order that the unities might be preserved, it was essential that all the individuals to be brought together in the group should be killed at the same season of the year. Nothing could be more ridiculous than to have the different members of this family group wear the coats of different seasons. A male in the summer pelage guarding a band in which the females should wear a January coat, while the kids were of the size and in the dress of early autumn, would excite the mirth of the hunter and would bring discredit on the museum where such an incongruous group was on exhibition. The difficulty of obtaining the specimens was therefore not the only one to be overcome. They must be secured at approximately the same season of the year.

SEPTEMBER 23, 1889, NEAR THE SIMILKAMEEN RIVER IN BRITISH COLUMBIA

The place where we camped on the river was about 25 miles below Allison and four or five miles above the mouth of Ashnola Creek. After my friend had sent me off with Chinook Tom, we set out to approach the game. At that time we had seen only two goats, and these were 700 or 800 yds above us, on the mountain side across the creek. To approach them it was necessary to go up the stream, cross it and then to clamber almost as far above them as they were now above us. Then working along the mountain side, until we were directly above, we could creep down to a low shoulder beneath which they were lying. From that point it was thought that we could get a shot. After following up the valley half a mile, we plunged down the steep hillside, crushed our way through the brush in the creek bed and began the ascent on the other side. Tom's moccasin-shod toes clung to the steep slope with a tenacity that I greatly envied, while my stiffer shoes slipped and sprawled and noisily hit against the rocks and trees in a way that must have been quite as annoying to my companion as it was to me.

At length, after many pauses for breath, the weary climb was over, and we passed out of the timber far above the goats. We could see them, still lying in the same place, on the other side of a wide ravine, thick with dead timber…which we must cross before we could descend to a point from which we could shoot. At the foot of a high cliff we stopped for a moment to rest. We had hardly seated ourselves when we saw two other goats come running out of the timber below those which were lying down. These two I at once recognized as a female and kid. Climbing steadily up the slope they soon joined the two which were lying down. These rose to their feet, and for a few moments all four stood looking out over the valley below them. Then they turned and began to clamber up the hill. At first, when the second pair of goats made their appearance, I had supposed that they had come up from water and would lie down with the others; but it was now evident that they had been alarmed by something in the valley and that all four were about to seek the heights for safety. They clambered up the side of the ravine until they had reached the shoulder from which I had hoped to shoot, and then, turning to the right, passed out of sight behind it, taking a course which led toward some vertical cliffs, which we had noticed from the other side of the stream.

As soon as they were out of sight, Tom and I started across the ravine, after brush and the slippery rocks made our progress slow and noisy. Having crossed, we kept down the other side until we reached the shoulder beyond which the goats disappeared. Here we found their tracks and followed them along the narrow ledges of the cliffs, under low-growing pines whose roots were thrust deep in the crevices of the rocks and over steep rock faces where the footing was very precarious. It was only now and then that tracks could be seen, for the trail along which the game was passing was so stony that often their feet left no imprint. Occasionally, however, a foot mark would be seen, or a fragment of rock freshly turned from its bed, would indicate the passage of some animal. In the excitement of the moment I gave no thought to the difficulties of the way, but later, after we had returned to the horses and I looked back at these cliffs, it seemed impossible that any creature except a goat, a mountain sheep, or a bird should have passed along them.

We had followed the scattered traces for perhaps half a mile, occasionally clambering up or down the cliff to look into some little pocket in the rocks, which might possibly harbor our game, when on a bit of soft ground we saw the tracks of several goats and felt sure that our band was still before us. A few moments later Tom, who was a little in advance, suddenly threw himself flat on the ground and excitedly whispered, "You see 'um? Shoot." I could see through a thick tree that overhung the trail a dim white shape, which could only be a goat, but I could not tell whether the animal's head or tail was toward me nor whether it saw us or not. Tom was so excited, however, that I felt bound to shoot. He wriggled about on the ground and kept whispering, "You shoot. You shoot." So though I could not myself see any necessity for haste, I took it for granted that the case was urgent. It was manifestly useless to fire through a mass of branches at a shadow, and I noiselessly scrambled up on a mass of rock lying above the trail. From this point I found among the branches of the tree an opening, through which I could get a clear view of a patch of white hair about three inches in diameter. At this patch I fired, and as the smoke cleared away I saw that the white shadow had disappeared.

Springing forward 15 or 20 ft. I passed the tree and had a clear view of the trail ahead. On a great rock, which was dotted with blood, stood a white goat with its head up and expressing in its attitude more alertness than I had ever before seen in an animal of this species. At the foot of the rock on the downhill side, standing on the slide rock of a little ravine, was another goat wounded, with its head down. These two, both old ones, were the only goats in sight. Of course, immediately after my shot I had slipped another cartridge into my gun, and the instant that I sprang into the open, the old rifle jumped to the shoulder and a ball tore through the heart of the goat on the rock. It half reared, fell over backward near its wounded companion, and went rolling down the hill over the slide rock. At the sound of the shot a kid, hitherto hidden behind the great rock, sprang into view on a lesser pinnacle. Again the fatal crack rang out, the kid sprang outward and downward, and tumbled over and over down the hill after its mother.

While all this was going on, Tom had appeared on the scene and was dancing about on a point of rock near me like—to use a vulgar but expressive phrase—a hen on a hot griddle. Little whoops and chuckles of delight sounded from him, and now, as he saw the wounded goat at the foot of the rock begin to hobble off, he called out, "Shoot 'um again." It seemed unnecessary to do this, for I could see that the first ball had ranged lengthwise through the body; but I neither wished to lose the animal nor to follow it far, so I shot it again. It joined the procession, which I could see out of the corner of my eye still tumbling over and over down the hillside.

But the end was not yet. Just as the last shot echoed among the crags, there dashed down the trail and into view about a point of rocks, another kid which had apparently started at the first alarm to climb the hill, but, finding itself alone, had come back to look for its mother, running to meet its death. It came bounding along from rock to rock with head erect, and quick, springy motions, resembling in its actions a mountain sheep far more than a sluggish goat. It ran quite close to me, and with a feeling of pity for the poor thing I killed it. There were no more.

Although so long in the telling, the time which elapsed between my first shot and my last was probably not more than a minute, perhaps even less, for I had loaded and fired as rapidly as possible, and there was always something in sight to shoot at.

To convey any adequate motion of Tom's enthusiasm and delight is quite beyond my powers. He danced, and gurgled and crowed like a delighted infant. For a little while articulate speech seemed to fail him, and he could only whoop and chuckle, and sing, and pat me on the shoulder. At last, however, he burst forth in praise of my shooting and of my gun: "Oh, you, Huyu, huyu good shoot. Get 'em all. O Skookum mushket. Good for goosly bear." And many other enthusiastic words.

As a matter of fact, I had done no good shooting. At that distance, and with the opportunities I had had, it would have been disgraceful to fail to kill as many of this little band as I had wished to. Tom, however, was probably accustomed only to guiding young men whose feelings overcame them at the sight of game and who shiver and tremble when they put their cheeks down against the stocks of their rifles. But young men require to be braced and supported before they can hit anything. Then they hit their game usually in the foot or in the ear, and sometimes even in the body. This last is rare. Tom's dealings I fancied had been with hunters of this class, and I was confirmed in this conclusion by a remark which he made that night in camp when he was detailing to the packers and other Indians about the fire the events of the day. He concluded his story by saying: "I have not seen a white man like him."

After all the goats had rolled down the hill out of sight I turned to the beaming Tom and asked him how many there had been. He replied that he thought there had been three; I told him that I imagined that there were four, but the whole thing had taken place so quickly that only a general impression of the number remained on my mind. The readiest way to learn how many there were was clearly to follow down the blood-stained ravine and count them. This we did, finding one old goat about half way down, and near the bottom in one pile three more. When they were counted there was more rejoicing from Tom, who was evidently well-pleased with his white man.

Victoria, B. C. Oct. 28th 1889

My dear Sir:-

I have shipped to the U. S. National Museum today by freight, Via N. P. R. R., a box which contains among other things material for the group of White Goats, (Mamza montana) about which Mr. Hornaday has so frequently written me during the past year or two:

The box ought to reach your museum within a month, I will write Mr. Hornaday and notify him of the shipment, and will enclose him the bill of lading, and Consular Certificate,

Yours very truly,

Geo. Bird Grinnell,

Mr. G. Brown Goode,

Washington, D. C.

George Bird Grinnell letter to Smithsonian. October 28, 1889 letter to Dr. Gerrit S. Miller Jr. *Smithsonian Institute Archives.*

To get the animals down to the creek bed, where we could take their skins off, did not occupy much time, and it was only 11 o'clock when we sat down to smoke a pipe before beginning this work. As each animal had to be measured with exactness, and the skins removed with peculiar care, this task took us about three hours. It was nearly 4 o'clock before we had packed the loads on the horses and started for camp.

My memory of the day and its events is still clear. I had been asked to get the material for a group and had the fortune on this first day's goat hunting to stumble on two nannies and two kids and to get them all in three or four minutes with four shots. The same day my friend [George H. Gould, who accompanied me on this trip] killed a billy, which I think completed the group.[82]

In a letter to Mr. W.T. Hornaday, Smithsonian Institute, I wrote: "My Dear Sir…I am glad to learn that the goat skins are in good condition and really think that I was very lucky to be able to get hold of this material in just the way I did. Thanks for what you say about the Museum's paying me for these skins. Of course I will not put any price on them, but if you think them worth anything I shall be glad to get it to help me out on the expenses of my trip, which were heavier than usual. The fifth skin about which you write belongs to my friend, Mr. Gould. He could not wish to *sell* it, although quite willing to give it up, if [used] for the group."[83]

Smithsonian Accession Card. *Smithsonian Institute Archives.*

6

1890

More Mapping and Discovery

Letters to Jack Monroe:

Jan 4, 1890: I had begun to think that perhaps you were dead, but it appears that you are only married.

July 18, 1890: I have not heard from you for quite a long time but I understand that you are ready for me whenever I may turn up.…I should want Billy Russell to go around with me and interpret [when I visit the Indians]. *If I do this I should want a horse to ride all the time.*

July 23, 1890: Your letter of July 8ᵗʰ reached me yesterday, and I am very glad to hear from you again, but sorry to learn that you are under arrest for disturbing the peace.…It is probable that I shall want to start for the lakes about the first of September. My plan, after we have reached the foot of the lower lake, is then to go up Kennedy's Creek to the glacier [at the head of the North Fork], *climb this ice and see what is to be seen on the mountain, then to come back down Kennedy's Creek as far as is necessary, to cross over the shoulder to Swift Current, up Swift Current as far on the north fork as possible to see what there is there, then to come back down to the old camping ground below the falls, up the south fork of Swift Current, up Cataract Creek as far as possible, and then, if necessary, cross over onto the waters running down to the St. Mary's Lake and follow them down to the lake.*[84]

SEPTEMBER 1–4

Left agency at 8 o'c. Rode to Two Medicine. Waited one hour when Schultz & Billy Jackson came down with a train. Jack still at their camp. I went up there and spent the night. Rode down to Indian Camp & found Jack there. Spent the day rigging pack saddles and getting ready to start tomorrow. Started about 8 with two packs; good road for 7 or 8 miles up ridge on N. side K's Creek, then struck timber. After striking timber we followed creek on base of Chief Mt. Camped after four on South end creek. In camp at dark.

SEPTEMBER 10

Started about 10 o'c for home camp. Crossed front of Mt. Robertson. Climbing above timber. A furious storm of wind & snow set in when we had reached top of Mt. and looked down into the deep rocky basins. A long, cold day during most of which we walked, leading horses. The wind so cold and furious that the horses would not face it but tailed toward it. We got down all right and reached camp about 3 o'c. Found G.H.G. who has been here 3 days.[85]

SEPTEMBER 15

At the foot of Mt. Wilbur, and lying against the [northwest side are] vertical cliffs which rise without a break thousands of feet above it, is a little glacier less than half a mile square, which is constantly pushing out into the lake. The waters carried by the eddying winds against this ice undermine it, and as this goes on, sections of the glacier fall off into the water, so that the little lake is dotted with a multitude of tiny icebergs which…glitter in the sunlight until at last they melt. [I named it Iceberg Lake.][86]

SEPTEMBER 18

About noon started for falls of Swift Current. Got tangled up in down timber and brush. My horse fell on me in down timber, bruising my leg against a log and holding me so that I could not get out without help. Very painful. Got to camp at six o'c.

Iceberg Lake. *National Park Service, West Glacier, Montana, Kiser, 1910.*

SEPTEMBER 19

Too lame to climb....There are two considerable masses of ice on head of main fork of S.C. above four [new] lakes. (Ed: These four lakes lie along the North Fork of Swift Current Creek. There were four other lakes first discovered in 1885 when entering the valley.) I named Swiftcurrent Glacier and Mountain.

SEPTEMBER 20

Jack and I climbed to the highest point...behind Rose Basin....A most superb prospect lay before us....We could see the heads of Kootenay, Belly, both Kennedy Creeks, Swift Current, Cataract Canyon and St. Mary's.... Glaciers were on every mtn. almost. A number of the mts. about the head of St. Mary's were very large. One [glacier] especially on S. Fork of St.

Swiftcurrent Glacier. *National Park Service, West Glacier, Montana, Elrod.*

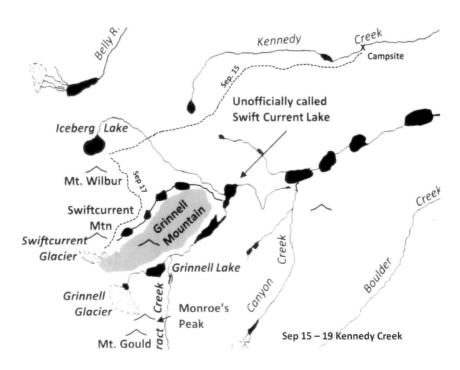

Blackfoot Glacier on Blackfoot Mountain. *Glacier U.S. Geological Survey, E.C. Stenbinger.*

Mary's, covers the whole mt., a very large one, from summit as low down as we could see it without a break. Took bearings on several mtn. peaks [for my map].[87]

We had no trouble finding a route to the top of the glacier and spent most of the day exploring it. We estimated its length to be several miles and its widest part more than two miles. We calculated the depth of the ice to be several hundred feet. That evening around the lodge fire there was considerable discussion of what the glacier should be named. Jackson suggested Pikuni, but Schultz thought its name ought to be Kutenay. [I] was of the opinion that it should be Blackfoot Glacier, since that would honor all three tribes of the Blackfoot Nation: the Pikunis, the Kainahs [Bloods], and the Siksikas, or Blackfeet proper. This name met with immediate approval… and the mountain on which the glacier lay was named Blackfoot Mountain.[88]

Letter to J.B. Monroe, February 25, 1892: The Blackfoot glacier is, I believe, about three miles wide and seven miles long; the greatest mass of ice and snow that I have ever seen.[89]

7

1891

Yale Men Can't Shoot[90]

Letter to J. W. Schultz, April 20, 1891: I don't know whether next summer will see me there or not. I want very much…to go up to the head of the St. Mary's Valley, above the Upper Lake. It will be rough traveling there and very slow, but I have no doubt that we could get there….The mountains on the south side of the Upper St. Mary's country….were covered with ice, and the glaciers there beat anything in the whole country….I would like to have you and Jackson talk this business all over and find out just what you are willing to do…[91]

~Bird invited Gould to join him again when he returned to the St. Mary's region in the fall.~

Letters to the Rhymer, May 20, 1891, and August 18, 1891: I will be taking a gun, but more than my gun will be my primitive surveying instruments, a surveyor's compass, and a primitive plane table. I want to take sightings of mountains. I fancy that mere force of habit will take me out to the Blackfeet reserve….As you know that Jack [Monroe] has skipped the country. I shall probably have to take Billy Jackson and Appekunny into the mountains with me—Appekunny to cook and Billy Jackson to climb the hills and carry my camera….[T]here remains the Upper St. Mary's, the country above the lakes, which I am extremely anxious to visit since I had a glimpse of it last autumn from the top of the high mountains back of Rose's Basin.[92]

The 1888 Yale Senior Class Skull and Bones Club, including Henry Stimson (*far left*) and William H. Seward III (*far right*). *Yale University Manuscripts and Archives.*

~In the summer of 1891, Bird planned the next trip to the St. Mary's Valley while dining with two New York friends, fellow alumni and law school graduates from Yale: William H. Seward III, grandson of Lincoln's secretary of state, and Henry Stimson, who was elected to Phi Beta Kappa while at Yale.[93] The two men became excited at Bird's description of the upcoming trip.~

> *Letter to Appekunny, Aug 1891: Mr. Stimson and his partner will take out with them a 4x5 Hawkeye camera with a roll, and I shall not pack along a camera.*[94]

~Bird invited his Yale friends to join him in the hunt. Needing another experienced hunter, he contacted Appekunny and invited him to contact Billy Jackson about joining him and his inexperienced hunter friends.~

In August, I left New York and reached the Blackfeet Agency September 1st. Here I met Schultz and Jackson, who Schultz invited to be our scout. I went to Billy Jackson's to stay. Henry Stimson and William H. Seward reached

Jackson's cabin on September 3rd. That evening we [moved to Billy's lodge and] sat around the lodge fire, eating and smoking. I asked Jackson to tell of Custer's disastrous campaign of 1876 and his own experiences in it as one of Custer's scouts. He related,

> *The scouts had urged Custer not to attack the camp of the hostiles, as there were far too many for him to fight, but he would not heed our warning. The night before the fight we scouts were feeling low, particularly Bloody Knife, a Sioux, who had long been with Custer. He sat before our fire, vacant eyed, face sad, and at last said to us, "My friends, I have been warned that I shall never see another setting of the sun; it is that tomorrow I die."*
>
> *Come morning, Custer split the command, ordered Major Reno to lead part of it, and us scouts to go down the Little Big Horn and attack the upper end of the hostile camp, and he with his companies started to circle and attack its lower end....Soon, out from the timber close ahead of us, singing [and] shooting, came hundreds of Sioux and Cheyenne, far outnumbering us. I saw Bloody Knife, riding close at my side, go down,*

Inside Jackson's Lodge (tepee). *Left to right*: Appekunny, Bird, Jackson and Stimson. *Photo by Seward, Seward House Museum.*

118

he was the first one of us to be killed, and brave Charley Reynolds, our chief of scouts, was the next one killed. Reno saw that there was one thing to do: retreat to the hills. As the bugler was sounding the call, my horse, shot in the lungs, squealed shrilly and ran, carrying me well into the timber before he fell.

I landed at the edge of a thick grove of willows and rose brush and had no more than crept into it than a swarm of the enemy began riding swiftly up past my hiding place....There I lay all the long hot day, knowing by the firing that Reno was making a stand somewhere up the valley. Came evening, and I saw a soldier moving slowly, aimlessly in the timber. I joined him, a private named Jones, told him that when it was fully dark we would try to join our command....

I led him down the valley, looking for dead [Sioux] Indians. Found some, got from them what I wanted: two light-colored blankets and two pairs of moccasins. We put on the moccasins...wrapped ourselves in the blankets, Indian fashion, and turned back up the valley. Jones was all trembly over what we were to attempt. We neared the line of watch fires, walking steadily, easily, hoping to pass them without being noticed. But when we were between two of the fires, a man at the one on our left called out, "You two there, who are you? Where going?" I can speak Sioux well, but my heart was hammering...as I answered, lightly, carelessly, I hoped, "Just us. Going up a little way to look where the soldiers are."

The man said no more. We kept on; began climbing the timbered slope; presently heard a number of Indians coming straight down toward us. We ran—I to the right—and I knew that Jones had gone in some other direction. I stumbled over a big fallen tree; I stretched out close at its side; I heard Indians coming toward me, knew that they had heard us running. Two of them came up against my tree, climbed over it close beyond my head, and I heard one say as they passed on, "Couldn't have been deer, not after all the shooting here." And then the other one, "None of us would be running in here; they must be soldiers that we have overlooked."

Soon after they passed there was some scattered shooting that enabled me accurately to locate Reno's position. I did not move until near morning, then began climbing the slope....I heard a sentry shout, "Hey, you down there, halt!"

"Don't shoot. It's me, Jackson, one of your scouts," I yelled as I ran on up! and was soon within our lines and was being questioned by our officers. Jones, about starved, did not join us until the following night, after the hostiles had fled.

Jackson finally said: "Well it is bedtime, so, as the Blackfeet say, Ky-I. I've finished." Young Stimson pled: "Oh no. Tell us more. Tell us about Custer!" But I said, "We have a hard day before us, a big glacier to visit. I think we should sleep."[95]

We started for the mountains going as far as Milk River, where we camped. The next day was very smoky because of forest fires. The atmosphere was so thick that we could not see the mountains at all....We finally reached the cabin owned by Henry Norris who was glad to see us and was very cordial.

On Saturday, September 5th, we set out along the mountainside for the Upper St. Mary's Lake. On Goat Mountain at different places two of the horses missed their footing and rolled down the mountainside from the trail but were not injured. After considerable labor we got them back to the trail. A little beyond here we camped in a fair camping place where there was enough level ground for the horses to feed and for us to make camp. The next day we started on, following the blazed trail made by the Kootenay Indians up the river....At last I went ahead and led the outfit down to the lake and out to the beach where we had fairly good traveling. At its head, the lake is wide and square. The Upper River is a rapid stream, 60 feet wide and 4 feet deep.

Working up the river we found that on our right, the northerly fork of the St. Mary's flowed into the main river from the west, and the southerly one from the southwest. A high-timbered mountain separates the two. The St. Mary's Falls are below the fork and hardly more than a mile above the lakes. Near the lake the river valley is low—nearly flat, thickly overgrown with willows and alders, and difficult to pass through....Towards the south side of the valley there is [a] little meadow of coarse slough grass, and in the timber there is some grass on which the animals fed. In this valley we put up the lodge and spent a good night.

Since nothing was known as to the way up the valley, we decided to remain in camp where we were and devote a day or two to picking out a trail before starting up the river. Seward and Stimson went to hunt goats in what is called the Colonel's Basin, a large rough basin in Goat Mountain, named for Colonel Baring of London who hunted in it the years between 1885 and 1890. The smoke was so thick, as it had been ever since we started, that it was impossible to see far, and this interfered with our geographical work—that is to say, our efforts to make a sketch map of this country.

September 7th. I started up the Upper St. Mary's Lake with Schultz and Jackson to look at a trail. We went perhaps six miles up the valley. As soon as

Right: *Rescue of a Pack-Horse from the Brink of a Precipice.* Century Magazine, *1901.*

Below: Campsite on Upper St. Mary Lake. *Seward House Museum.*

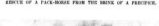

DRAWN BY DE COST SMITH.   ENGRAVED ON WOOD BY C. W. CHADWICK.

RESCUE OF A PACK-HORSE FROM THE BRINK OF A PRECIPICE.

St. Mary Falls. *Glacier U.S. Geological Survey, Tim Rains.*

I came to the bank of the river I noticed the milky appearance of the water and concluded that there were one or more glaciers at its head. The fall of the river is rapid, with many cascades and much swift water. The forks are about three miles above the lake. The North Fork is much smaller than the main stream, and its water is clearer.

The following day we moved up the [south fork of the] river, but we made only seven or eight miles for the travel was very slow and laborious....The going was difficult for horses and for men. In fact, there were points where we had to leave the mountain and go down into the valley and there struggle with mire and brush. However, we finally reached the foot of the glacier....I named the glacier, Stimson Glacier, and its mountain, Stimson Mountain. (Ed: The mountain peak named Mount Stimson was renamed Mount Logan, and the photograph of Mount Stimson is the currently named mountain, which has no glacier, on the southern portion of the Continental Divide.)

The next twenty-four hours were cold and wintry with abundant rain. I climbed the moraine which lies to the west of Stimson Glacier and came down another moraine further to the west. I estimated the Stimson Glacier as a mile wide and three quarters of a mile deep. It was steeply

Stimson Mountain. *Ron Casey, Helena, Montana.*

sloping and extensively crevassed and broken. Below it is a large waterfall. It was from this camp that Seward, while climbing a mountain in search of goats, and with his gun on his back because he was obliged to use both hands in climbing, met face to face a white goat that was coming down the mountain. They were hardly more than ten feet apart when they saw each other. The goat got out of sight before Seward could free his gun.

On September 11th, while Seward and Stimson went hunting, Jackson and I climbed a high mountain to get some courses for the map. Two or three miles southwest of their camp they noted on the skyline a large V-shaped notch which looked promising. As they approached it they found unmistakable evidence of an old trail with cuttings on many of the stunted trees to mark it; the trail led directly to the notch....When they returned to camp, Grinnell pointed out the notch's similarity to the rear sight of a rifle, and the tip of the west-side mountain just showing beyond, it is like a front sight. When he called attention to this, there was general agreement on the names Gunsight Pass and Gunsight Mountain, and it followed that the lake on which they were camping should be Gunsight Lake.[96]

Gunsight Mountain, Lake and Pass. *National Park Service, West Glacier, Montana.*

We reached camp without trouble about 8:30. I repaired the sights of my large rifle. The next morning Jackson reported that we had consumed all our provisions except for enough to carry us for about four days, and we moved camp to Gunsight Lake. Seward and Stimson went ahead with the purpose of hunting goats on a tall, pinnacled mountain. We followed with the train and made camp about three o-clock....About sunset we heard shooting on the mountain above the camp and could see where the young men were shooting at goats on the rock far above them. They fired fifteen or twenty shots at long range but killed nothing. The goats apparently had never heard guns before, and they did not know what the noise meant. The two goats at which they were firing became confused and jumped about not understanding the dust and sounds of the balls which struck near them. One goat refused to run until he had been shot at six or eight times. He then climbed, but only slowly.

Letter from William H. Seward III to Bird Grinnell, March 1, 1918: I have taken great pleasure in seeing some of the modern maps with the names given by you on our trip to many of the mountains, glaciers, and streams. Fusillade Mountain recalls especially amusing memories, as I recall the number of shots Stimson and I wasted in shooting upwards at a group of goats just before the sun set, without even disturbing them, and the laugh we received from you and Billy Jackson on returning to camp after

Camp at Gunsight Pass. *National Park Service, West Glacier, Montana, Elrod 2198.*

midnight....On greeting our return, you then and there gave the mountain across the valley the name of Fusillade Mountain.[97]

The following day Jackson and I climbed the big timbered shoulder that divides the north forks of the St. Mary's River from the South Fork.

Letter to J.B. Monroe, December 8, 1891: I got up to the head of the St. Mary's River after many tears and much profanity, for the way was very rough. At the same time, the distances are short, and it only took us two whole days travel to get from camp at the head of the Upper Lake to the glaciers at the head of the South Fork of the Upper St. Mary's. It was about as rough traveling as I have ever seen. Down timber, mire [and] rocks, and worst of all the brush is as high as a man's head and so thick that a horse will not face it.

Fusillade and nearby mountains. *National Park Service, West Glacier, Montana, Hileman photo.*

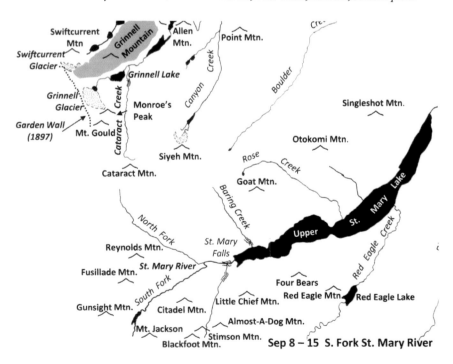

The slopes were very steep; we had to cross one snow slide and many growths of alders. We reached the foot of the mountain about noon and presently began to climb it, reaching the top just after three o-clock. The time of climbing was two hours and forty minutes. [I told Jackson that I was going to name this mountain after him.] (Ed: Blackfoot Glacier lay in the saddle between Blackfoot Mountain and Jackson Mountain. By 1914, Blackfoot Glacier's recession had resulted in two distinct glaciers. The western portion, which lay on Mount Jackson, was then named Jackson Glacier, and the name was not officially recorded until 1929.) From the top we could see a fine park-like plateau with short crisp grass and little clumps of timber running out from the foot of [a tall mountain]. We had a fine view of the North Fork and the mountains all about them. Of these mountains the most imposing I named Mt. Reynolds for Charles Reynolds of *Forest and Stream Publishing Company*.

It was 4:30 before Jackson and I started down the mountain, and when we reached the horses we felt doubtful whether we could get into camp that night. We tried to find better traveling on the way home, but we got into a perfect confusion of downed timber, alders, and vine brush. We fought through this until dark, and then, finding a level place where we could tie our horses and another little spot for a fire, we made the best of what was bad.

Mount Jackson. *Blake Passmore, Kalispell, Montana.*

Mount Reynolds. *Blake Passmore, Kalispell, Montana.*

The night was warm, and we were quite comfortable. At daylight we set off again and reached camp about nine o'clock, tired and hungry.

After eating some food we prepared to move....During the night the horses had found the baking powder can and had eaten all our baking powder. No more biscuits! Our sugar had already been consumed, and the food left consisted of flour and bacon. After a long hard day through the brush and down timber, we camped about five o'clock at the camp and occupied a little lagoon on the south fork of the river.

The next day [September 16], we made a fairly early start and reached Henry Norris' cabin about sundown. The following day Seward and Stimson set out for the Kutenai Mountain while I remained at Henry Norris' cabin to do some writing. It was on this day, September 17th that I made in my notebook this entry:

> *How would it do to start a movement to buy the St. Mary's country, say 30 x 30 miles, from the Piegan Indians at a fair valuation, and turn it into a national reservation or park? The Great Northern Railroad would probably back the scheme, and Senator T.C. Power would do all*

he could for it in the Senate. Mr. Noble might favor it, and certainly all the Indians would like it.

This is the first suggestion, so far as I know, made towards setting aside the St. Mary country as a national park.[98] In a 1927 letter from me to Mr. R.S. Yard, Dept. of the Interior, among other things I informed him:

These mountains were then a part of the Blackfeet reservation, but I felt sure that the Blackfeet would be willing to sell the mountains to the government, for the Blackfeet had always been a prairie people and had never been mountain hunters. The only Indians who hunted in these mountains were from outside the Blackfeet reservation, namely Crees, Bloods, and Kutenays from west of the continental divide.[99]

The following day [September 21], with Henry Norris, I rode up on Flattop to pass around behind Singleshot and traced the course of Boulder Creek. Had a long, hard day, most of it occupied in walking and dragging our horses. My horse, while passing over a steep slope, got the rope of the pack horse under his tail while on the slide rock of Flattop. [He] began to buck, and got his legs tangled up in the rope. He began to stagger. I jumped off, alighting on my head, and turned half a dozen summersaults down the steep hill. Caribou, my horse, fell with a resounding thud just as I got up. I cut my head a little and bruised and scraped both my legs, but the horse was not hurt. During the day we made the round of the plateau. It rained and blew so that we got wet, and the temperature fell until it was very cold. We went down into Singleshot Basin and built a fire and cooked some coffee and meat. Then we started back to the cabin. We had intended to stay out over night, but the adverse weather conditions made us decide to return.

During the morning I worked on my map, and in the afternoon with Henry Norris went out in his boat to take the course of the lake.…[We] crossed the lake nearly opposite Red Eagle Point. Here we landed and walked up to the mouth of Red Eagle Creek which empties into the lake near the end of the point. I took the course of the upper part of the Upper Lake which is, by compass, due southwest. The bend begins…at the point of Red Eagle Mountain.

On the return trip the wind was still higher and the lake rougher. I estimated that the waves were eight or ten feet high from trough to crest, and they followed one another very rapidly. The little skiff rode them well, but it was hard to hold straight. We found we could not reach the outlet

Mount Norris. *Blake Passmore, Kalispell, Montana.*

directly; the wind and waves broached the boat and she partly filled. We drifted ashore, scrambled out, turned out the water, and ran her off again. Henry jumped in and pulled to the outlet. We reached the cabin about 5:30, cold, wet, and hungry.

The next day we started for Red Eagle Lake in the afternoon.

~At this time, Bird spotted a mountain peak due south on the Continental Divide and named it Mount Norris.~

After we had reached Red Eagle Valley, Henry lost the trail. [He] took us too far up on the mountain, and, because of the rough going, we had to stop when darkness fell. We lay on the mountainside within half a mile of camp which we could not reach because of the danger of injuring the horses.... We could hear the camp bell all night. Fortunately we had our bedding with us in the packs, and so we slept comfortably, though the night was cold. The next morning we found an easy way down to camp.

September 22nd was rainy and no one went out except two or three anglers....The next day we returned to Henry Norris' cabin. The day after reaching the Norris cabin Seward and Stimson went with Henry to the Kutenai Mountain for a last hunt—which was unsuccessful.

Swiftcurrent Creek downstream from Swiftcurrent Falls. *Author photo.*

~Stimson went to the railroad on September 25. Seward, Appekunny and Grinnell left for Swift Current. With the departure of Stimson, Grinnell was able to undertake what he referred to as "his work." This comprised two activities, the first of which was to visit or revisit the areas shown on Grinnell's 1885 map of the St. Mary's Lake Region and complete the mapping as accurately as possible.~

We camped below the falls on Swift Current [Creek]. The next day we passed a recently-abandoned camp where five lodges of Indians had been. These may have been the Stonies reported by Dutch Louis. A wonder: On this day there was no wind, and the lakes, without a ripple, were more beautiful than ever. On the way up Swift Current I passed close to a hawk-owl sitting on a tree—the first one I had ever seen alive. A walk in the afternoon showed two or three goats on the high and distant mountains, plus a brood or two of Franklin's grouse.

The following day Seward and I started on foot for [a huge mountain to the east of Mount Gould], and after some hours of slow, bad climbing we found ourselves in a pretty little rock basin. Across this basin feeding on the slide rock, was a goat which we hunted with success. Seward killed

Seward's goat (posing). *Seward House Museum.*

Mount Allen From Swiftcurrent Lake. *Eric Kendall, Many Glacier Hotel.*

him after eight shots. This goat was photographed lying down in a good position. Cutting it up, we started down the mountain in the middle of the afternoon. Seward carried the hide, fat, and one shoulder. I carried the hams and saddles, say 50 pounds to each load. After difficult climbing down bad ledges and passing through much timber and wading many creeks and swamps, we reached camp shortly after dark, very tired and lame. Seward's letter recalled:

> *I, of course, remember being with you on Cataract Creek, and the incident in naming Mount Allen, where we killed a mountain goat.... The reason for my suggesting the naming of the mountain after my sister was because she and I have always been the greatest companions. The mountain was named after my sister, Cornelia Seward Allen, and if I am not mistaken, she still has the goat skin and head which I had made into a rug for her upon my return. My sister, as you know, is a direct descendant of my grandfather, William H. Seward, Secretary in Lincoln's cabinet. She still has the goat skin and head which I had made into a rug for her upon my return.*[100]

The next day was spent in camp resting. Jackson came in about noon with a fresh supply of provisions. We had a feast. The next day we decided to move up the valley of Cataract Creek. It was there that I first beheld a beautiful mountain at the head of Cataract Creek, which I named Cataract Mountain [which we climbed]. I saw one old camp and took bearings to various St. Mary's & Swift Current points. The head of Cataract Creek and [the] head of [the] northernmost fork of North St. Mary's are separated only by a thin wall of rock. [To the north, looking toward Chief Mountain, I also viewed a reddish-rock mountain and ridge which I subsequently named Seward Mountain and Seward Ridge to honor Lincoln's secretary of state and, consequently, my friend, his great-grandson.] When we reached the head of the lower of the two lakes it was about dark, so we camped about where Jack Monroe and I camped the first time we visited my glacier in 1887.

It was now October, and bad weather was to be expected at any time. During the day it snowed quite frequently, and we spent most of the time in the camp. Jackson told some more good stories, among them one about the Flathead woman who made it rain when the Bloods were attacking the camp. Of course, in ancient times when they were using bows and arrows, rain during a battle wet the bow-strings which, when wet, stretched and became practically useless.

Cataract Mountain. *Blake Passmore, Kalispell, Montana.*

The snow and the cold weather make hunting on the steep mountainsides difficult. The water from the little spring freezes and the snow conceals the rocks and ice over and among which one must climb....There was a heavy wind during the afternoon and the snow was slowly disappearing—evaporating rather than melting.

The night of October 4th was cold, but the morning was bright and clear.... At a distance in the snow on the sides of the mountains were seen a number of trails made by sheep or goats. Some of us clambered up to the basin between Mounts Allen and Cataract and hunted on the mountains. Schultz and I climbed high on Cataract Mountain to look for some recognizable landmarks to the south.

We tried the two low passes on either side of Mount Cataract but could see nothing. Long clouds streamed off to the eastward. Two high mountains on the south side of Cataract Creek hid the country beyond. Seward and Jackson climbed as high as we did and were further back from the ridge. They were not bothered by clouds and could look over a low wall to the south from which they recognized the St. Mary's Lakes, Blackfoot Mountain, Mount Jackson, Mount Gould, and the low dividing shoulder of Mount Reynolds. They could see our old camp and other recognizable points. They saw two wild sheep. Fresh sheep trails were abundant on Cataract Mountain, and we might have killed something if we had had time to hunt. By continuous climbing, Schultz and I reached the top at four o'clock and started back at five. We got to the horses about dark at the same time as the others. Going down the stream we lost the trail, blundered into some down timber, and got into camp late.

The next day with Seward and Schultz, I climbed Grinnell Mountain, reached the summit about one o'clock, and took a number of courses to distant recognizable mountains. We saw two goats, one of which Seward killed....We saw wolverine tracks on the hill. It was almost dark when we reached camp.

On October 6th I climbed Mount Allen with Seward and Schultz. We saw a goat lying on a ledge just above the slide rock on Mount Gould, and Seward tried to get it. He fired ten shots and probably all of them at more than 150 yards distance, but the animal got away.

We found, and looked down into a remarkable hole in the mountain just north of the summit. It is the head of Canyon Creek and is perhaps two thousand feet deep with straight walls. At its head there was a small glacier from which the stream flows for a few hundred yards into a lake, half a mile long and very narrow. The stream flows in a northerly direction with a bend to the eastward. The rolling hills of the lower Swift Current country can be seen down the stream.

The next morning we moved down to the falls. Some of the men went hunting but saw nothing....On October 8th we went down to Norris' cabin which we reached about dark. [His cabin] was occupied by some soldiers from Company C, 1st Cavalry. They were very pleasant and turned out in order to make room for us....Our courses on the Swift Current Valley [north of Grinnell Mountain] showed that it bears nearly west, 90 degrees north true. From the mouth of Boulder Creek to St. Mary's, the distance is about one and a half miles.

The next day we returned to Cutbank Creek, reaching Jackson's cabin about seven in the evening. Hugh Monroe, Billy Jackson's grandfather [and first white man in this area], says that in the old times when game was so much more abundant, white goats were very plentiful in the mountains, but even then they always lived high up. None of the Indians killed them except the Kutenays, who like the flesh....In the old times when the Piegans were camped near this butte, he had climbed up to the top of it with a lot of other young fellows and driven the sheep down to the plains below where

Billy Jackson's cabin, his family and Hugh Monroe. *Montana Historical Society.*

the people were waiting on horseback. On such occasions they used to kill hundreds of sheep for their skins which were used for making war shirts, and for women's dresses.

Our team of men with outdoor experience accomplished much on this trip; however...nothing but Billy Jackson's good nature and my profanity pulled us through....Appekunny looks back on the trip with entire disgust for the reason that nothing was killed except 1 sheep and a goat or two, and, as he wrote to Jack Monroe, "we lived principally on mush and glaciers."[101] We hunted successfully in order to maintain fresh meat for our meals. I was able to name several features and map much of the area in both the St. Mary's and Swift Current Valleys and to take courses on distant, but known mountains for my map. Billy Jackson and Schultz scouted the areas we needed to visit in order to allow me to make my field maps. Billy Jackson and Hugh Monroe educated us in the ways of the Blackfeet Indians.

~All in all, 1891 will be looked at as a beneficial year. The explorers parted ways, each to his own home, with Bird's destination being an office in downtown New York City.[102]~

1892 EFFORTS TO PROMOTE GLACIER NATIONAL PARK

Letter to R.W. Gilder, Century (Magazine) Company, May 12, 1892: *For the last five or six years, I have been spending two or three months each season in the northwestern corner of Montana.... This country has never been mapped, and no one has ever been as far back in the mountains as I have. For the last two or three years I have devoted myself mainly to securing material for a map.... The scenery in this section is wonderfully grand; the mountains high and remarkably bold, and on the north side of many of them lie great glaciers.... I write to ask whether you would care to have me call sometime and show you the photographs from which you could decide whether it was worthwhile to do anything in this matter....*

Letter to William H. Seward Jr., May 25, 1892: [It is] *possible that what I write may not be satisfactory to the editors of the* Century Magazine....*so say nothing about it....I should like to have the knowledge of my failures confined to as small a number of people as possible.*

Letter to G.H. Gould, November 30, 1892: Century *has accepted an article of 9–10,000 words on the St. Mary's country, to be illustrated with photos and my map....* [T]*his article will not see the light before mid-summer. It certainly seems to me as if it were a summer article since it deals with snow-covered mountain peaks. (Ed: In fact, it was not published for nine years.)*

Letter to C.C. Buell, Century Company, December 15, 1892: Mr. Colton, who is drawing [my] *map, wants to know what space it will occupy in the magazine.*[103]

8

1895

Agreement to Purchase Blackfeet Mountain Land

Letter, July 11, 1895, from GBG to Secretary of the Interior, Hoke Smith: In response to your telegram, I do not covet a place on the said commission, but I feel I should accept if it would be helping the Indians toward self-support and civilization.

Letter, July 17, 1895, from GBG to Wm. Jackson: I feel I can do more for the tribe on it than off it (the commission). One of the first things the commission should do is go up into the country and look at the minerals, taking 2–3 weeks. I would like you and Jack Monroe to guide us. I want to see justice done, but also their (the Indians') ideas of the value of this land are very much exaggerated. I hope the Indians can be cared for another ten years at a fraction of what they are getting with the present treaty.[104]

~In his master's degree thesis, Christopher S. Ashby detailed the history of the Blackfeet sale of almost one million acres of their reservation back to the U.S. government:~

In January of 1895 Agent Lorenzo Cooke, acting on orders from the Commissioner of Indian Affairs, called a meeting with the leading men of the Blackfeet Reservation. He wanted to discuss with them the possibility of selling the western, or mountainous, portion of their reservation to the Government. The Blackfeet voted 16 to 5 to negotiate a sale of the Reservation's western portion to the Government. The Blackfeet requested that their longtime friend, George Bird Grinnell, be a member of the negotiating committee....The Secretary then appointed Walter M. Clements [a lawyer from Georgia], William C. Pollock [of the Indian Bureau], and George Bird Grinnell to serve as the members of the commission....The party set out for the Blackfeet Reservation, arriving there on August 30, 1895....The commissioners expressed a desire to hear from as many of the Indians as possible. Mr. Clements said that in dealing with the Indians it was not the intention of the commission to obtain a bargain for the Government, but rather to buy the unwanted land for the price that the land was worth. He further stated that it was the commission's duty to be fair to both the Indians and the Government. Commissioner Clements sprained an ankle when he jumped out of a wagon and landed on a pile of rocks and was not able to participate much in negotiations. Thus, only Grinnell and Pollock made the inspection trip into the mountains.[105]

SEPTEMBER 1

Rode with Pollack to look at cattle to be issued to Blackfeet.

SEPTEMBER 20

[Blackfeet] councils…come to nothing as yet.

SEPTEMBER 21

Indians want two million and told it is absurd. Two councils met.

SEPTEMBER 23

Morning council took 1 hr. 45 min. Indians late, adjourned with advice to Indians to be prompt in the future. Reassembled at 2 P.M. At 1:45 every man in his seat. Little Dog demanded $3,000,000. Refused. Speeches till dark. All [Indians] firm in declaring would not take less than their price. Commission offered 1 million if southern boundary is GNRR mainline, or 1¼ million if southern line is for the land north of Birch Creek. At end Little

Dog declared useless to meet again. Commission hinted would leave the next day. By 9 P.M. Indians were sorry for their folly and desperately afraid lest we should go away. They asked advice of the Major [Blackfeet Indian agent], then sent for the commissioners and asked for us to come in and shake hands. Indians will spend tomorrow counselling among themselves.

SEPTEMBER 24

The Indians are talking.

SEPTEMBER 25

Council set at 10 A.M. and everybody was ready to talk. White Calf [chief of the Piegans] asked for 1½ million for all the mountains south to Birch Creek. We accepted and read our memo of agreement. Everything went swimmingly….After lunch we had a discussion and finally agreed on treaty. In the afternoon it was accepted and tonight everybody is glad. Many Indians made good speeches to me, thanking me.

Mr. Pollock…said that in general the terms of the Agreement would be the same as those of the Agreement of 1887, and that money owed the Blackfeet would be paid in ten yearly installments. Anticipating a successful session, a rough draft of the Agreement had already been drawn up. Pollock then read the draft to the Blackfeet.…The Blackfeet agreed to this method of payment and the signing ceremony for the agreement was set for the following day.[106]

ASHBY CONTINUED, "ALL OF the adult male Blackfeet on the reservation were urged to be present for the signing of the Agreement. The commissioners, Indians, interpreters, and other interested parties gathered at 10:00 a.m. on Thursday, September 26, 1895, to listen to and sign the final draft of the Agreement of 1895.…The Agreement was read to them by George Bird Grinnell. The Agreement was interpreted to the Blackfeet.…The Agreement was then signed by the three commissioners, 306 Blackfeet, witnesses J.E. Webb, R.B. Hamilton, James Willard Schultz, and the three interpreters. Indian Agent George Steele also signed the Agreement, and certified that the total male population on the reservation was 381."[107]

September 26

Agreement read, voted on, carried unanimously. Signing began at noon. By night had over 200 (Piegan) signatures.

September 27

Continued signing. 273 signatures by night. Sent news story (4000 words) to [*Great Falls*] *Tribune*.

September 28

Signing continued. [Over 320 signed.] Dance that night. Packed during day and started for Blackfoot Agency 9 P.M. Left 1:40 A.M. with Conrad.[108]

> *Letter, November 6, 1895, GBG to Wm Jackson: I am pleased with the bargain made with the Indians. It was liberal on both sides. If Piegans continue as they have in the past five years, they will be the richest tribe in the country and will have a large sum to their credit. It depends on the agent and how funds are administered.*

1896 to 1907—Mining Failures

~On June 10, 1896, the agreement was approved, as written, by an act of Congress.[109] In 1897, by the official initiative of the U.S. Forest Commission a large section of this mountain country was set aside and named the Lewis and Clark Forest Reserve by direction of President Cleveland. The rest of the land was thrown open in April 1898.~

Ashby further wrote: "The opening of the land was followed by a great incursion of miners and by a general prospecting on both sides of the mountains. Beautiful samples of copper were found, brought out and exhibited, and on some veins much work was done....Experts from important mining camps were brought to the newly-opened mining territory and looked it over, but all shook their heads and none seemed to agree with the local optimists who declared that this was to be a 'bigger camp than old

Butte.' After two or three years of unsuccessful prospecting for gold, silver, copper, and oil the miners who worked in this region became discouraged, and practically all the claims were soon abandoned. By 1902 almost all of the last discouraged prospectors had withdrawn from the region, leaving behind them no marks of their presence more permanent than the prospect holes or shafts which they had dug at the cost of so much labor."[110]

~There was an organized effort to find oil in the valley. The oil exploration was completely finished by 1907. By 1910, for all intents and purposes, the mining and oil exploration efforts in the ceded strip were finished.~

9

1897

Over the Garden Wall

Letter to Edgar Hough, April 1, 1897: I know all about Schultz, Jackson and Kipp, but I must say that Jackson has always stood well up to the collar when he has been with me in the mountains. Schultz, of course, is not worth anything except as cook, and he irritates me even in that humble office.

Letter to George Gould, July 8, 1897: Jack Monroe and I started from the railroad for the St. Mary's Lakes and then to the extreme head of St. Mary's River, and there, being specially favored by Providence, made a quick rush and climbed Mount Jackson, probably the highest peak in that section of the Rocky Mountains. This was a great triumph, and was a pure piece of luck.

While on the summit with Jack, they saw a huge glacier on the southwest slope of Mount Jackson that they named Harrison Glacier after Frank Harrison, a rancher from Babb and a friend of Jack's.

When we got up to our usual camping place we found the ground covere by about 10 feet of snow; had to tie our animals to the pine trees; made an early start next morning; climbed the mountain in seven hours; got back to camp in about 10½ hours; packed up and went down to the valley below where there was feed for the animals. On our way up Jack and I were swept away by the water in the North Fork of the St. Mary's River. Jack lost his

Harrison Glacier. *Glacier USGS, W.C. Alden.*

Westside View of the Garden Wall. *Author photo.*

axe and the thumb nail of his right hand. I lost my gun, overcoat, various small articles of clothing, and for quite a long time my breath. For the rest of the day we were, of course, very wet, and matches and tobacco pretty well soaked, so that we could not smoke which was a deprivation....[We were] soused about in the tumultuous waters, sometimes right side up and sometimes wrong, until at last we had drippingly crawled out on either shore and counted up our bruises. [After a few days, we returned to the Agency where Indians were camped in the circle getting ready for the Medicine Lodge ceremonies]...stayed 4 days....the last day of my stop there I was highly honored by being promoted to the head chieftainship of the tribe, being saluted as the Father of the People [by Chief White Calf] who had adopted me into the tribe.[111]

~Months later, Monroe sent Grinnell a letter stating that he found his axe, gun, overcoat and other things.[112] On a trip later in 1897, after visiting the Blackfeet to obtain information for Bird's book, another little group was camped next to Grinnell Lake. Don Robinson wrote,~

"One evening, around a campfire, they were singing the then-popular song, 'Over the Garden Wall', when one of the party remarked, 'There is one wall we cannot get over.' The name was immediately applied to the ridge—The Garden Wall."[113]

10

1898

Who Is the Biggest Man?

Letter to George H. Gould, June 20, 1898: I leave in 2–3 days for Montana. I shall not carry a gun, or even a fishing rod but shall take an alpine stock, and have a try at Blackfoot Mountain. Jack, and possibly Deming, the artist, will accompany me. [I also took Stimson's level.]

Letter to J.B. Monroe, November 11, 1897: Did you, Stimson and Pinchot climb Blackfoot Mountain? If so, was it higher than Jackson?

Letter to J.B. Monroe, December 15, 1897: Pinchot told me that Blackfoot Mountain still remains unconquered. Until somebody goes up that, I shall still regard myself as chief of the St. Mary's country.[114]

The winter of 1897–98 had been very severe in northern Montana, and more snow had fallen in the mountains than for many years before. Spring had been late this year, and the snows had really scarcely begun to melt before summer. [N]ow in mid-July the streams were bank-full and were rushing torrents....This year, therefore, we two, who had been swept away the summer before [losing axes, guns, clothing and so on], promptly shied [away] when we came to the water, and after a mile or more of difficult uphill travel found a crossing where we forded the stream with entire comfort....[T]he northwestern bank of the stream was followed...until nightfall, when we camped in the thick timber....By half-past ten the next morning, after an exhausting struggle, we reached the edge of timber line and there pursued our way over the snow fields along the mountainside by well-known trails to the old camp on one of the streams which have their heads in the Blackfoot glacier....At 6 o'clock the next morning, Jack and I, armed with ice axes and a coil of rope, set out to see whether a way might be found to the summit of Blackfoot Mountain, which had long been the goal of...at least [one] of the party....

[F]or years it had been my special ambition to climb Mount Jackson and Mount Blackfoot, the two highest of them all. In the summer of 1897 Jack and I had made a quick run to the head of the river...[and] had succeeded... in reaching the summit of Mount Jackson....The Blackfoot Mountain lies further back than Jackson...and since to reach it the great Blackfoot Glacier must be crossed (an ice river which might present all sorts of difficulties and perhaps even force us to turn back) it seemed a much more desirable peak to conquer than had the nearer and really more imposing Mount Jackson.

To men whose legs for a year past had only been accustomed to gripping the flanks of a horse, the climb upward, among the dark firs [and] over the frozen snow banks, seemed long and tiresome....[W]e began to study the great ice field before us in order to discover the easiest path to the peak of the Blackfoot Mountain....[I]t could be seen that the face of the glacier was very steep and that one or two long crevasses stretched out nearly...across it....[T]here was good going in the direction of the main mountain peak; and...to push for the lower end of this shoulder seemed the better policy. So we set out for the lowest point of this ledge.

For the next three or four hours we had monotonous but easy climbing over the gently-sloping surface of the glacier. The old snow upon its surface was soft enough to give good footing [and] was not very slippery....At length we reached the border of the glacier, and [by grasping] the rocks, pulled ourselves up, and took our way along the gentle ascent of the shoulder.... Here, before long, we came upon the fresh track of mountain sheep going in the direction we were pursuing, but nothing living was seen. Almost at the crest of the shoulder we sat down and took a long rest...

In the next half-mile lay, perhaps, the only dangerous part of the climb. Here the ice field fell away sharply, and we were working across it at right angles to the direction of its slope. For 1,500 or 2,000 ft. below us this slope continued or grew steeper, and then there was an abrupt fall into a rock *couloir* [corridor] far below. If one had slipped on the traverse, he would have [awaken] in another state of existence. The rope now came into play, and tied together we made a progress which was still more slow and careful. One man usually had his ice axe firmly planted in the hard snow before the other moved. It was really a relief to reach the edge of the glacier, and to be treading once more on solid earth and stone, steeply sloping though it was....

[W]e toiled up the steep mountain side...pulling ourselves up over tiny precipices. As we neared the summit nothing was to be seen under foot or about us except these great masses of lichen-covered rocks. We scrambled up over the last of these, and when only a few feet below the [summit], Jack, who was in advance, with a fine courtesy and a thoughtfulness that would be matched in few companions, stopped, turned to me & motioned me to go ahead. It was a touch of delicious generosity which gave an insight into my friend's character; for as I have already suggested, to me it did me a little something to place my foot first on the summit....Half a dozen steps more brought us to the mountain's crown, and as we lightly hurried on to the very highest point, all the labors of the morning seemed to us as nothing. As we stood upon the top, however, my heart was in my mouth for a second or two, for there before us was a huge stone freshly turned over. Could it be that other people had already been here, and had begun to build a monument on the summit? A second glance, however, served to show that the stone had been turned over by a bear in his search for mice.

After the first hasty survey of the country, we sat down and smoked and talked, and in a general way located all about us the different landmarks that we knew....The spirit level (a geological instrument), when used, showed Mount Jackson to be very slightly higher than the Blackfoot Mountain....All the other mountains were, as Jack remarked, "mere holes in the ground."...[After descending the mountain] we reached camp late that afternoon and found that the artist [Deming] had made an effective study of Mount Jackson.[115]

Letter to Grover Cleveland, August 5, 1904: ...attempted a climb of Mt. Jackson....Made a quick climb to the timberline with Jack, camped overnight, started before daybreak and reached the summit....When we got around to the north we saw there a big mountain, higher than anything else in sight—for the Rockies at this point do not attain a great elevation. This mountain we had never seen before and it was evidently nameless. We asked each other what we should call it, and after a little discussion I said, "Here, that is the biggest mountain anywhere about here, and Cleveland is the biggest man in the country; let's call it Mount Cleveland." Jack, who is a good Republican when it comes to voting, said, "Cleveland it is!"

Mount Cleveland.
*National Park Service, West
Glacier, Montana.*

~Over the past thirteen years, Grinnell and companions had named over forty geological features, and Lieutenant Beacom had named two more "Grinnell" something-or-other. Only Monroe's Peak and Point Mountain were later renamed by the USGS. (See appendix.)~

Letter to George H. Gould, August 20, 1898 ... [D]*id I tell you that North is married? It was a great shock to me to find here on my return, an invitation to his wedding, and it seems melancholy that an old fellow like this, after having travelled the prairies for so many years—for he is older than I am—should be at last roped, thrown and tied. However, he seems to feel no mortification over it, and writes to me quite cheerfully. I do not, therefore, venture openly to offer him my sympathy, but I feel for him deeply.*

11

1901

Crown of the Continent, September

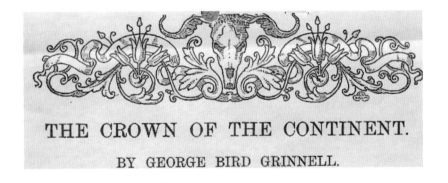

THE CROWN OF THE CONTINENT.

BY GEORGE BIRD GRINNELL.

Far away in northwestern Montana, hidden from view by clustering mountain peaks, lies an unmapped corner—the Crown of the Continent. The water from the crusted snowdrift which caps the peak of a lofty mountain there trickles into tiny rills, which hurry along north, south, east, and west, and growing to rivers, at last pour their currents into three seas. From this mountain peak the Pacific and the Arctic oceans and the Gulf of Mexico receive each its tribute.

Here is a land of striking scenery....If one turns his back upon the prairie and looks west and south, the view is barred by a confused series of unknown mountains. Here are canyons deeper and narrower than those of the Yellowstone, mountains higher than those of the Yosemite. Some are rounded and some square-topped, some are slender pinnacles, and others knife-edged and with jagged crests, each one a true sierra. Many are patched with snow, and the highest wear their white covering from year's end to year's end. Along their...slopes, slow-moving ice rivers still plow their deliberate way, relics of mightier glaciers, the stiffened streams of which in a past age fashioned the majestic scenery of today. These

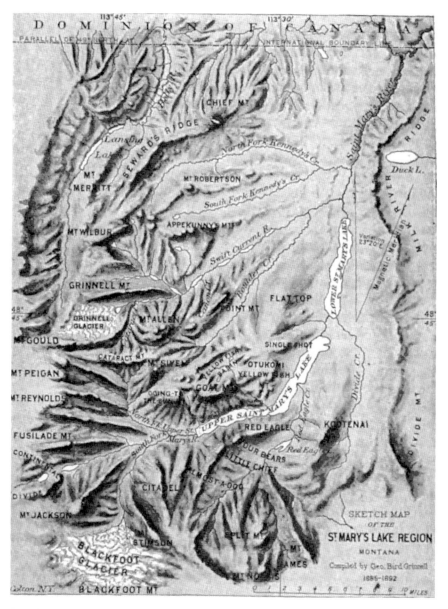

Final Sketch Map. *National Park Service, West Glacier, Montana.*

Century Magazine, *September 1901.*

old glaciers dug out for themselves channels between the mountains, and, when the ice melted, left deep canyons, the walls of which sometimes rise vertically from three to four thousand feet....In the dense forest a few moose, elk, and deer still exist, and...bears prowl through the timber, tearing to pieces the rotten logs for worms, or turning over great stones to find the ants and beetles on which they prey. On the high lands game is more abundant. The cliffs are still climbed by the nimble sheep and the sure-footed white goats, and there is no reason why the hunter should starve. During the migrations there are swans, geese, and ducks in great numbers; five species of grouse are found on the mountains; the streams and lakes swarm with trout and whitefish; and in early autumn the hillsides are covered with huckleberries....

Persons who have given intelligent study to the problems of forestry and the needs of the arid West appreciate the importance of protecting the sources of rivers flowing from the Rocky Mountains over the plains east and west, and it is obvious that the greater the number of settlers who establish themselves on these dry plains the more water will be used and so the more needed.

Happily, in 1897, by the official initiative of the United States Forest Commission...a large section of this mountain country was made into a forest reserve, including Upper St. Mary's Lake. Under faithful and intelligent supervision, the dangers above spoken of will in large part be obviated, and in due time Montana will rejoice...that so large a source of her water supply has thus been preserved for her people.[116]

~This article was Bird's first effort to inform the public about the natural beauties of this area. He hoped to persuade the public to preserve this wilderness from uncontrolled visits by hundreds or thousands of citizens by establishing a national park.~

Letter to George Gould, September 6, 1901: Many thanks for your polite remarks about "The Crown of the Continent"...which was submitted in the winter of 1892 or '93. They must have wanted it to bake a little longer before they published it (in the next Century).

Letter to Francois Matthew, USGS, December 12, 1901: The map in the article in Century Magazine contains errors. I did not see a proof of the article which was written nearly ten years ago....In the time which elapsed between the writing...and its appearance, I had learned enough about the region to have corrected the errors.[117]

Return to St. Mary's

Letter to H.L. Baldwin, USGS, December 2, 1901: I recently spent two or three weeks…part of the time on the head of the St. Mary's River… and a part on the head of the South Fork of the Swift Current, near my glacier.… [W]*hile at the head of the Swift Current, my brother-in-law, Newell Martin and I climbed Mt. Gould.…We crossed the Continental Divide at the northwest arm of my glacier, following the cliffs around behind my glacier, and finally ascended the main peak of Gould where we built a very small monument.*

Letter to George Gould, December 6, 1901: [We reached the] *head of main St. Mary's River without doing anything very noteworthy. Then we went to the head of the South Fork of Swift Current, camping in the usual place below the upper lake, and one day started from that camp at 7 o'clock and climbed up on to my glacier, up to its western arm through the sag behind my mountain, across the Continental Divide, and then southward behind the peaks that lie west of my glacier, and finally reached the base of Mt. Gould, ascended it from the west and reached the summit about 7 p.m. Turning about we started for camp and traveled through the night until 3 a.m. when the moon set. We were then tangled up on a series of ledges about one mile from camp, and being unable to find our way in the dark we sat on a ledge by a small fire until daylight came, and reached camp about 8 o'clock in the morning. I confess that I was tired. Between Oct 11 and Oct 28 we were without a single stormy day—neither rain nor snow. I carried no gun, but we succeeded in having Ashbel Barney kill a billy goat of satisfactory size. We saw about 20 sheep, 30 goats and 3 bears which we bombarded at a distance of 700 yards—ineffectively of course.*

1902, Elizabeth Curtis Williams

Letter to Hamlin Garland, April 2, 1902: Mrs. Williams will go to Colony (Oklahoma) in 2–3 weeks to take a lot of photographs for me [among the Cheyenne].

Letter to Rev. W.C. Roe, April 5, 1902: Thank you for the arrangements you made for Mrs. Williams.

Letter to George Bent, April 5, 1902: Hamlin Garland, a friend, is coming to Colony, and next week, another friend, a woman is going out there to take some photographs. Her name is Mrs. Williams, and if you see her I wish that you would help her if you can. She wants to take pictures of people doing the regular things that they all used to do in the old times. She wants to see the women dressing hides and packing wood, and water, and putting up the lodges, and packing the horses, and doing a great many other things that they no longer do. These photographs, I hope, will go in my book of the Cheyennes when it is finished.

George Bird Grinnell and Elizabeth Tepee. *National Park Service, West Glacier, Montana.*

Letter to Major G.W.H. Stouch, April 7, 1902: Please see that she has a room, perhaps in the girl's building, and that she is properly introduced at the mess.

Letter to Major G.W.H. Stouch, July 28, 1902: Some of Mrs. Williams' pictures are coming out very nicely.[118]

~On August 21, 1902, George Bird Grinnell (fifty-three) married Elizabeth Kirby Curtis (twenty-four), widow of Emery Leverett Williams of Boston, who accompanied him on practically all his western trips in his later life. She was a photographer and frequently photographed the Cheyennes and Blackfeet.[119]~

JULY 10

We started at 7:30 and the 4 tourists rode to back of Mt. as far as horses could go. Then on foot went farther behind and climbed to saddle. Then up slide rock to comb...reached summit after some labor...The women climbed with extraordinary pluck and facility. At the very first they had a little difficulty, but in a very few minutes Elizabeth came to understand how to walk and balance.[120]

Campsite at Chief Mountain. *National Park Service, West Glacier, Montana, Elizabeth Grinnell Photo.*

155

Letter to George H. Gould, August 21, 1903: We climbed Chief Mountain in the company of Jack [Monroe] *and Billy Upham,* [and] *a man and two women, Mr. and Mrs. John J. White and Mrs. Grinnell, where, I suppose, no woman has ever been before.*

Letter to L.H. North, December 23, 1903: The Cheyennes call me Wikis, meaning "bird" (not my name but that "I come and go with the seasons.")

12

1907–1910

The Legislative Process

Great Falls Tribune *editorial, October 3, 1907: During Pinchot's recent visit (Gifford Pinchot, U.S. Forest Service) he said the park would probably occur if favored by Sens. Carter and Dixon and Mr. (Congressman) Pray.... [W]e think that they will make a capital mistake if they do not give the project enthusiastic support.... [A]* few can enjoy it as a National Forest Reserve by obtaining land and building a summer home.... but ten thousand would find enjoyment in these things if good roads were built and the scenery were made accessible at a moderate cost.... *[T]he country belongs to all the people of the United States and a broad, unselfish spirit of patriotism and citizenship should dictate a policy that would make the country accessible to the most people. A national park would undoubtedly serve that end.*[121]

Letter to Robert Underwood Johnson (editor), c/o the Century Co., 1907: About 10 years ago the Century *printed a story of mine called "The Crown of the Continent."... Three or four years later* [actually six years] *Senator Carter, after much persuasion, introduced a bill.*[122]

"I have been trying to get Senator Carter to introduce a bill for a good many years, and at last he has done it."[123] The start of legislative action began on December 11, 1907, when U.S. Senator T.E. Carter of Montana introduced a bill, S. 2032, into the Senate to set aside the area as a National Park. The bill was considered to have several undesirable clauses and returned to

Carter for rewriting. Senator Carter immediately revised the bill as suggested and again presented a new bill, S. 5648, to the Senate on February 24, 1908. On March 6, 1908 I wrote to Madison Grant, conservationist and Secretary of the Boone and Crockett Club, to present a resolution to the members showing support of the Senate bill to create Glacier National Park.[124] During this same time I wrote dozens of letters, asking the recipients to write to Senator Carter…to arouse in his mind sufficient interest in his own bill to get him to push the bill to a vote.[125]

The bill was approved in the Senate and sent to the House of Representatives in May. Here Congressman Charles N. Pray guided it through the Committee on Public Lands of which he was a member. The Committee reported it back to the House with the recommendation that it be passed. The House took no action on it, and the bill died.

On June 20, 1909 Carter introduced a third bill, S. 2777, to the Senate. It lay in the Public Lands Committee until January 23, 1910 when it was reported *out* by Senator Dixon of Montana. It was agreed to on February 9. It went again to the House of Representatives where it was agreed to with amendments. These amendments gave control to the Secretary of the Interior, among other provisions, to develop rules and regulations for preservation and protection of fish and game, and to issue permits for removal of mature, dead, or down timber. Here Congressman Pray, along with several others, fought very strongly to get the bill through the House.

It was then returned to the Senate where that body objected to the House amendments. It was then given to a conference committee for adjustment of the differences. The committee reached a compromise, and the bill was finally presented to the House and agreed to without a record vote. On the same day it was presented to the Senate which also agreed to it. From there the bill went to President Taft who signed it on May 11, 1910, bringing Glacier National Park (the 8th national park in the U.S.) into existence.[126] The following year the Montana Legislature ceded exclusive jurisdiction to the area to the United States. The next day I sent a letter to Congressman C.N. Pray, Montana: "[H]earty congratulations on the signing of the Glacier National Park bill. The passage of this measure is a great triumph for you, and for the Montana delegation, and I believe that succeeding generations will rise up to bless all who had a hand in forwarding this bill."[127]

Passed Senate, [illegible]
Public Lands Committee [illegible]
15-1910

Union Calendar No. 152.

61st CONGRESS,
2d SESSION.

S. 2777.

[Report No. 767.]

IN THE HOUSE OF REPRESENTATIVES.

FEBRUARY 10, 1910.

Referred to the Committee on the Public Lands.

MARCH 15, 1910.

Reported with an amendment, committed to the Committee of the Whole House on the state of the Union, and ordered to be printed.

[Omit the part struck through.]

AN ACT

To establish " The Glacier National Park " in the Rocky Mountains south of the international boundary line, in the State of
Montana, and for other purposes.

1   *Be it enacted by the Senate and House of Representa-*
2   *tives of the United States of America in Congress assembled,*
3   That the tract of land in the State of Montana particularly
4   described by metes and bounds as follows, to wit: Commenc-
5   ing at a point on the international boundary between the
6   United States and the Dominion of Canada at the middle of
7   the Flathead River; thence following southerly along and
8   with the middle of the Flathead River to its confluence with
9   the Middle Fork of the Flathead River; thence following the
10   north bank of said Middle Fork of the Flathead River to

1910 S. 2777 House of Representatives Tentative Act. *Yale University Manuscripts and Archives.*

Grinnell's pivotal role in the creation of Glacier is indicated by an extant letter written by Montana representative Charles N. Pray. The congressman just had concluded directing the final enabling act through the House and a joint Conference Committee.

Dear Mr. Grinnell,

I have been notified by telephone from the White House that the President had just signed the Glacier National Park bill. The bill has now become law and I sincerely hope that someday in the near future, when you are in the West on your summer vacation, that I may have the great pleasure of meeting you in the new National Park.

With many thanks for your assistance in creating a sentiment favorable to this measure...

13

1910–1915

Park Improvements[128]

Letter to L.H. North, June 13, 1911: I want to see Glacier National Park for the last time before it gets full of wagon roads and hotels.

Letter to J. B. Monroe, March 14, 1911: I hope the Indians can be hired for work on the St. Mary's Canal as they were [hired] on Two Medicine Ditch. They work faithfully…purchased their supplies from the Reclamation Store, made money, and might have saved some.

AUGUST 9, 1912

Riding up to Flat Top [with Lute] and met a party of three horsemen. The leader spoke and at length asked if this was Mr. Grinnell's party and if I was Mr. G. Just before we turned off to [Lake] McDermott, they stopped again, and the leader introduced himself as Mr. Louis (Lou-EE) Hill (president of the GNRR).

AUGUST 23, 1912

To the hotel to talk with Supt. Chapman. While there Mr. Louis Hill with Mr. Noble [of GNRR] & half a dozen others came up in an auto.…They need 2,000,000 ft. of timber for their construction work. This to be taken from the Park and perhaps Indian Reserve. Unless they log with discretion they may do much to mar the beauty of the Park, which, according to this story, is to be turned into a series of storage reservoirs and logging camps. Utilitarian Americans![129] (Ed: Most lumber, and logs for hotel lobbies, were brought by railroad flatcars from Oregon and Washington.)

1—U.S. GOVERNMENT

Letter from R.A. Ballinger, Secretary, Department of the Interior, to GBG, January 17, 1911: …in the Sundry Civil Act. Approved June 25, 1910, an appropriation of $15,000 for the improvement of Glacier National Park and the construction and repair of trails and roads therein.…Major William R. Logan is the designated acting superintendent.

~In its publication, "The History of Glacier National Park," the Great Northern Railway provided insights into some early efforts of the park rangers that were necessary to be accomplished under extremely dire conditions and with little financial assistance from the U.S. government:~

"[On] August 8, 1910, Major William R. Logan was commissioned to head the affairs of the park.…There were practically no roads and little equipment.…Major Logan organized a patrol of six rangers and for the following winter each was assigned a section of the park boundary to patrol. The next summer they began to build a headquarters, a few roads, and to extend a telephone line.…They were responsible to patrol winter and summer from small crude cabins. They traveled their beats alone, and many accidents and even deaths resulted from these lone patrols through

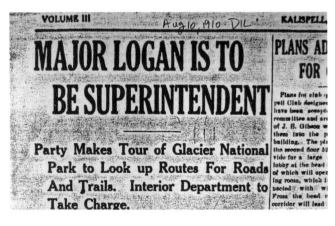

Major Logan announcement. *From the* Kalispell Daily Inter Lake *newspaper, University of Montana Archives.*

the mountains. One ranger froze to death on the trail between cabins on the east side of the park; another was buried in a snow slide for twenty-four hours yet managed to dig himself out and work his way back to his station; still another slid down a snow bank and broke his hip, which resulted in a grueling two-day trip back to his cabin, unaided."[130]

Letter to R.T. Evans, topographer, USGS, February 2, 1911: I am grateful to your organization for retaining most of the names I gave to various natural features.

Letter to W.R. Logan, Park Superintendent, May 16, 1911: I am hoping to get out to see you again soon and to see what is happening in the country which I felt for many years was my private estate.

Letter from W.R. Logan, Park Superintendent, to GBG, May 23, 1911: [The Corps of Engineers] *will be building a macadamized road from Belton to Lake McDonald 24 feet wide…clearing and widening trails as snow clears.…Trail over Swift Current up St. Mary's via Red Eagle, taking in glaciers,* [will be built and] *cut out the old Two Medicine trail and make that connect with the Red Eagle and Cut Bank trails on the west side.…By the first of July, I hope to have the trails all in fairly good shape.*

Letter to Henry Gannett, chairman, U.S. Geographic Board, June 12, 1911: ..Almost-A-Dog was named after one of the finest and most delightful of Blackfeet old men.…It means literally almost a dog from a dream of a man who saw a strange creature that was "almost a dog."

~The Department of the Interior was working closely with and through its superintendent to improve the park for visitors. In 1914, after three years of effort to make the park visitor-friendly, the department released a twenty-six-page General Information bulletin prior to the arrival of guests in 1914. The Great Northern Railway was embarking on a major construction activity to create hotels and chalets to house and feed guests. Bird was involved with all parties, requesting information and providing clarification on a number of issues which pertained to the park.~

2—GREAT NORTHERN RAILWAY

Michael J. Ober, in his book *Glacier Album*, explained why the Great Northern Railway had an interest in a national park: "Officials in the Great Northern Railway's headquarters in Minneapolis aimed at promoting the new park in order to increase rail passenger activity. They believed that other transcontinental railroads had profited by having a national park adjacent to their lines....Great Northern officials had lobbied hard to move the enabling legislation forward to create Glacier National Park, and they were expecting to reap the rewards."[131]

~Bird had known James J. Hill since 1891. When they first met, he explained to Hill his vision to have the area adjacent to and north of Hill's mainline become a national park. Sensing a business opportunity to create a lucrative tourist destination for his railroad passengers, Hill was on board. It was Bird's hope that Hill and the railroad lobby in Washington, D.C., would help in convincing Congress that this area should be set aside for the benefit of the people. Soon after, Bird met Hill's son, Louis W. Hill, the president of the line. In later years, both James and Louis Hill of the Great Northern Railway discussed with Grinnell their plans to build Swiss/Alpine-style hotels and chalets within the park boundaries. Bird recognized that people would visit this area in droves, so he grudgingly endorsed the Hills' idea for appropriate accommodations in the park.~

HOTELS AND CHALETS

~After the president signed the bill that created Glacier National Park, the Great Northern formulated plans for developing the area to receive visitors. It had already begun designing facilities and roadways which would be needed for the influx of expected visitors. Almost immediately, trains began hauling building materials to the areas where hotels and chalets were to be built. After offloading these materials over many months at both Belton (for the western buildings) and Glacier Park Station near Midvale (for the eastern buildings), primitive roads and horse-trails were cut to allow moving the material to the sites of the hotels and far-off mountain chalets. Construction began on the Glacier Park Hotel near Midvale and on the chalets at St. Mary Lake, Many Glacier and Two Medicine. The Belton Chalets were completed in 1910. Tent camps were soon provided to allow visitors crude accommodations beginning in 1911. These were eventually replaced by the Swiss-alpine log buildings at nine camps throughout the park. The immense Douglas fir posts in the Glacier Park Hotel were hauled in by trainloads from western Washington and Oregon, from one to three on one flat car, and were moved to, and erected on, the site, which was only one hundred yards from the station. The Glacier Park Hotel was first to be opened for visitors in 1913 and was augmented with an annex completed the following year.

During the winter of 1913–14, John Lewis built the sixty-five-room Lewis Hotel (now the Lake McDonald Hotel) near the site of the original Snyder Hotel. The logs for the Many Glacier Hotel had to be hauled by horse teams from the Glacier Park Station to the hotel forty miles north over primitive trails, and wagons filled with other building materials similarly used these trails to deliver to the building sites—the chalet facilities and the hotel. The chalets were completed between 1910 and 1914 with the distant Granite Park chalets completed in 1915. The Many Glacier Hotel was the last hotel to be opened for visitors in 1915. In 1917, the operation and management of these accommodations were turned over to the newly formed Glacier Park Hotel Company. ~

Glacier Park Hotel, 1913. *Yale University Manuscripts and Archives.*

Many Glacier Chalets. *Seward House Museum.*

National park historian Joseph Sax said, "The railroads were a happy choice as concessionaires, for they had the capital to build...and they could look to passenger fares for their profits, rather than to exploitation of the park's natural resources. Hotels and restaurants could be run at a loss, and often were, and still the concession might prosper."[132]

~By 1915, a few future expansions and improvements still needed to be made. Distant areas where chalets would be built were economical for hikers and horse riders who were initially housed in the tents, which were a canvas imitation of the Blackfeet tepees. The future buildings' locations were modified by Hill based on previous bad experiences caused by avalanches and other weather-related occurrences, due to inappropriately placed buildings.

But the crown of Hill's vision was the Glacier Park Hotel, which became the headquarters for the hotels. The hotel lobby was characterized by two rows of sixty-foot-long, thirty-six-to-forty-two-inch diameter Douglas fir logs that supported the majestic ceiling.

Glacier Park
Hotel Lobby.
*Great Northern
Railway
Historical
Society.*

Finally, in 1915, the Many Glacier Hotel was completed at the shore of Lake McDermott (in 1929, officially "Swiftcurrent Lake") in sight of Grinnell Mountain and the southernmost finger of my glacier. Trails would eventually be cut so hikers and horseback riders could visit the glacier.~

PARK SADDLEHORSE COMPANY

~Louis Hill ensured his visitors access to many destinations deep within the interior of the park, by conveniently placing the chalets and hotels only a day's ride apart for horseback riders. Saddle horses were the best way to visit the interior of this one-million-acre wonderland. In 1912, the first saddle horse concession was organized, and the following year, William and James Brewster *from Banff received a one-year contract to provide horseback excursions. In the meantime, enamored of the idea of tourist buses, Louis Hill was having discussions concerning using the newly constructed roads as a testing ground with Walter White of the White Motor Company of Cleveland, Ohio. Hill recognized that tourist buses would become more practicable for most hotel visitors. In 1915, a new Park Saddle Horse Company, organized and owned by a Kalispell lawyer, was contracted to provide horseback trips into the interior of the park with a different chalet as each day's destination. This contract remained in effect for three decades.~*

ROADS

~With supplies and building materials needed to construct accommodations at eleven sites, and with visitors coming to stay at the two new hotels and nine chalets when they were completed, the Great Northern ran into a transportation problem. There were no roads to the distant chalets and hotels. Since the Glacier Park Hotel was only one hundred yards from the Glacier Park Station, the transfer from the train to the hotel was easily remedied with horse-drawn wagons and a few motor vehicles. The real problem would be to get passengers to the chalets and to the Many Glacier Hotel forty miles distant. Congress had appropriated only $15,000 for maintenance—of everything. The railroad spent its own money to cut trails for horses to the chalets to bring supplies and visitors and for roads to bring supplies and passengers to their appropriate destinations. The first road was constructed by a contractor between Midvale and the Many Glacier Hotel (the predecessor of the present Blackfeet Highway) in 1911. Those with automobiles who wanted to visit both sides of the park had to transport the vehicle on a flat car and family in a passenger car. This situation was alleviated in 1930 when a road was opened (now Highway 2).

In 1911, the first private automobile appeared in Glacier National Park (on the west side). On the east side, the first automobile to be driven over the newlyopened road into Many Glacier was one carrying Louis W. Hill and party on August 7, 1913.~

Louis Hill. *Minnesota Historical Society, Louis Hill Photo.*

Glacier Park Transportation Company

~The Glacier Park Transportation Company was founded in 1914. It had financial backing from Walter C. White of the White Motor Company of Ohio. He became the sole supplier of buses to the GPTC. His first buses had long (140-inch) wheelbases. Their gears were difficult to shift, requiring double-clutching, and the drivers were known as "gear-jammers" due to the grinding sound resulting from shifting the four-speed transmissions. The first tour buses seated seven passengers. There were ten buses, five touring cars and a couple of trucks. Years later, due to the increased number of guests in the hotels, a seventeen-passenger tour bus replaced the older models. When asked by Walter White what color Louis Hill preferred for the newer model of bus, Hill reached over to an ashberry bush, removed a sprig of red berries and said, "Paint them this color!"~

First tour bus. *National Park Service, West Glacier, Montana.*

Seventeen-passenger tour buses. *Robert Grinnell photo..*

BOATS

~The first boat, a steamboat, to carry guests and supplies on one of the lakes was operated in 1895 by George Snyder, who had built the Snyder Hotel on Lake McDonald. By 1910, Great Northern had upgraded to operating five boats on the lake. On Lake St. Mary, it launched a forty-foot twenty-passenger boat in operation between the town of St. Mary and the Going-To-The-Sun Chalets at the upper end of the lake. The next year, two more boats were added to supply and transport passengers to the Sun Camp. Finally, boats were launched on Two Medicine Lake and McDermott Lake (later named Swiftcurrent Lake).~

GLACIER PARK INDIANS

~The advertising department of the Great Northern Railway hired dozens of Blackfeet Indians to greet passenger trains in full native dress and accompany passengers to a tepee in front of the Glacier Park Hotel, where they told Indian stories and explained how implements on display were used. They traveled with GNR executives to national expositions to create a sense of the Wild West within the park. The Indians were referred to as "Glacier Park Indians," not Blackfeet Indians, and were instructed to wear not their own traditional "stovepipe" headdresses but to make and wear headdresses of other Plains Indian tribes. One story of the Indians is told of Two Guns, eventual chief of one of the tribes and son of White Calf, the chief of the Piegans. When meeting visitors during the Great Northern exposition in Washington, D.C., one year, he was approached by a U.S. congressman who gave Two Guns his business card. Two Guns reached into his pocket and retrieved an Indian head nickel, gave it to the congressman and said, "Here is my card."~

WELL, BIRD, WHAT DO YOU THINK?[133]

Letter to L.O. Vaught on July 30, 1912: I am perfectly free to acknowledge that in the case of the Glacier Park I foresaw a great deal of what has now come to pass, but, perhaps, I did not foresee it all. I knew, however, that if this was made a National Park that fact would mean my practical expulsion from the region, but I reasoned that the suffering of one or two unimportant individuals ought to weigh nothing against the possible delight of a thousand or hundred thousand other individuals who would enjoy

Glacier Park Indians. *Great Northern Historical Society.*

looking at the mountains and who do not know that such pleasures exist as you and I formerly enjoyed in these wild countries.

Letter to Daniel Doudy, Park Ranger, April 26, 1912: I understand that they have dotted hotels pretty much over all the Park, and I shall not greatly enjoy seeing them; but after all, that is what the Park is for—the benefit of the public—and those of us who knew it in its old wild days are a very small portion of the public.

Letter to Daniel Doudy, May 21, 1912: I suppose before long the Glacier Park will be run over by a lot of new people, and they will be telling you and me all about the country. In fact, I have already met one or two persons who described it to me and told me that I ought to go see it.

Return to Visit the Park[134]

July 30, 1913

Wired Glacier Park Hotel for room and seats on motor launch on Lake.

July 31, 1913

Good night and good breakfast. By automobile [from railroad station] to St. Mary's. Trip made in about two hours and comfortable....Everybody here is growling about the Gt. Northern Co. which they say is not willing that anyone else should make a dollar. The Ry. Co. wants to make it all—which seems natural enough.

August 1, 1913

A tourist caught tonight on a light rod a lake trout which weighed 24 lbs. on the store scales.

~After three days in Swiftcurrent, traveled to St. Mary's Valley.~

August 6, 1913

The basin of Red Eagle glacier deserves a better description than I have given of it. It descends from foot of glacier by a series of limestone terraces, up over which in many places one may ride a horse and finally falls away over a wall 1000 or 1500 feet high down which plunge two great waterfalls from the main glacier.[135]

Back in New York[136]

Letter to Charles Reed, Michigan, September 29, 1913: We spent a week or 10 days at the Glacier Park, and spent four or five of them with Henry Norris at the head of Red Eagle Creek. [On August 6] we climbed the hill which you and Mrs. Reed knew so well, and camped immediately under the glacier. The effort of climbing the hill and some carelessness about her eating, laid Mrs. Grinnell out, and before long we had to turn about and slide down, and took the automobile, if you please, for the big hotel [Glacier Park Hotel].

Letter to A.C. Stohr, December 24, 1913: It is, of course, a lovely country, but how much better it was before the public got into it. That, however, is a selfish way to think of the matter. As things are today, thousands enjoy it against tens that went there in the earlier days.

Letter from J.B. Monroe to GBG, April 18, 1914: On April 18, 102 sheep in sight at one time at Lake McDermott-Swift Current Falls; Kennedy's Creek, saw 60 in sight at one time; On Chief Mountain and back saw 22 sheep. 35 or 40 sheep can be seen at Swift Current Falls now....Saw at Iceberg Lake 25 or 30 goat; on Grinnell Mt...saw 25 or 30 goats.

1914–1916 Trips to the Park[137]

Letter to T. Elwood "Billy" Hofer, August 26, 1914: There is still quite a little room in the Glacier National Park that has not been invaded by the tourists. Of course, when you go along the main-travelled routes, you are pushed off the trail every few minutes by the multitude, but you can turn off some little side valley and in fifteen minutes' ride can get away from these people and go up some point in the hills where the tourists never come.

~In an interview on June 15, 1956, Mrs. George B. (Elizabeth) Grinnell told representatives of the National Park Service:~

"After the establishment of the park in 1910, regulations were set up to control travel into the more dangerous areas. On one occasion [in 1915] a park official who did not know of Dr. Grinnell's intimate knowledge of the terrain told him that he could not make a certain trip without a guide. Mrs. Grinnell recalls proudly that her husband immediately telegraphed Washington and word came back promptly that he was to be allowed to go "anywhere in the park he pleased."[138]

~Bird continued to make annual trips to Glacier National Park, and Elizabeth often accompanied him. When staying in the park, they often checked into the Many Glacier Hotel, which was conveniently located close to his glacier.~

Many Glacier Hotel invoice. *Yale University Manuscripts and Archives.*

Letter to L.O. Vaught, November 4, 1915: I saw the Park from its beginnings and since, I spent ten days or so in it this summer, stopping at a modern hotel and living the precise life of the average tourist, except that I did not hurry about as they do....I went into the Park, lived at the hotels, taking each day an all-day ride, and then came out again. I saw goats aplenty and tried to get back to where the sheep were in August, but I had hardly been out of my chair for a year or two and lacked the legs needed to take me up over the high ridges and to get back to the summer range of the sheep. I did not see one sheep.

I was much interested in the character of the people seen at the hotels. Among them there were a great many people of high intelligence and very just views. All of them, of course, were enthusiastic about the region.

JULY 26, 1917

E. greatly tickled because a Mr. Adams to whom she spoke asked if she was Mr. Grinnell's daughter or his granddaughter.[139]

14

1923

Visit to the Park with Elizabeth

SEPTEMBER 6, 1923

We left New York City by train to travel to Glacier National Park.

SEPTEMBER 9, 1923

We arrived at the Glacier Park Hotel. I saw Bull Calf who wants to hunt in the Park, but I recalled the treaty on the ceded strip which allows hunting according to State game laws. He had no license....We could not remember things alike....E. and I left for Many Glacier at 1:45....Later I saw Jack [Monroe] at St. Mary's....Later at the hotel I met the hotel manager, a Park Ranger, and Mr. Crawford who was in charge of the saddle horses.

SEPTEMBER 12, 1923

[Took] a short walk with E. Saw Canada jays and a kingfisher.

SEPTEMBER 13, 1923

Started before 8:30 for my glacier. Mr. Heilman, the photographer, had two large stout camera cases which he carried on a pack horse, led by a park guide....Elizabeth, by chance, rode Fish, a horse she has had many times at

George Bird and Elizabeth Grinnell. *National Park Service, West Glacier, Montana.*

Many Glacier....[At the] S. side of L. Josephine, crossed at its head, climbed the trail and had lunch at the spring. Began the climb. The trail was very steep in many places but the footing good. I had to stop rather often to get my wind. At length the three young men stopped at a point on my lake to take a picture of the falls and E. and I went on toward the ice. We kept on quite steadily, reached and climbed the terminal moraine, and sat down to await the others. Presently I went on under the lateral moraine—between it and the ice—and found a small black cave under the recently-piled-up glacial debris at foot of lateral moraine. Then I went back to E. who felt no disposition, as she said, to go further. I told her that she must at least stand on the glacier. Presently the others came up and we all went on it together. The cave was disappointing but H. (Heilman) took a number of pictures of different individuals in front of it. Later we crossed the glacial stream, got on the ice, [and] walked slowly and carefully up to its highest point. [Heilman took Elizabeth and GBG's picture.][140] Beyond us, halfway across the glacier from N to S is a deep, wide hollow, and under it was a deep valley into which the ice has sunk. Here were several seemingly unfathomable potholes to which the water from the melting ice was pouring. The amount of water lost daily from the ice is stupendous. We did not find the ice caves the photographer wished to take and don't know where they are. They were [previously] photographed by Mr. Elrod, a Missoula professor, and I am promised a copy of the pictures. I might send Heilman my photo of ice cave by Seward [in 1891] and get him to copy it.

While on the glacier, we saw 5 goats appear on the face of N end of Garden Wall: 2 nannies, 2 kids and a yearling. Later on the way down we saw other groups [of goats]: 4, 3, and about a dozen high up.

SEPTEMBER 14, 15, 16, 1923

We left in the morning to travel to the reservation....The next day we made a trip to inspect Indian farms....[T]he following day left for Sheridan before returning to New York.[141]

1924 Observations About the Park

Letter to L.O. Vaught, July 30, 1924: If we had not succeeded in getting these regions set apart as National Parks, by this time they would have been, in many cases, cut bare of their timber and dotted with irrigation reservoirs; the game would have been all killed off; the country would have been burned over. I am perfectly free to acknowledge that in the case of the Glacier Park I foresaw a great deal of what has now come to pass, but, perhaps, I did not foresee it all. I knew, however, that if this was made a National Park that fact would mean my practical expulsion from the region. I reasoned that the suffering of one or two unimportant individuals ought to weigh nothing against the possible delight of a thousand or hundred thousand other individuals who would enjoy looking at the mountains and who do not know that such pleasures exist as you and I formerly enjoyed in these wild countries.[142]

15

1925

Theodore Roosevelt Medal for Distinguished Service

MAY 1925—THEODORE ROOSEVELT DISTINGUISHED SERVICE MEDAL

You were with General Custer in the Black Hills and with Colonel Ludlow in the Yellowstone. You lived among the Indians; you became a member of the Blackfeet tribe. Your studies of their language and customs are authoritative. Few have done so much as you, none has done more, to preserve vast areas of picturesque wilderness for the eyes of posterity in the simple majesty in which you and your fellow pioneers first beheld them. The Glacier National Park is peculiarly your monument.[143]
—President Calvin Coolidge

Letter to L.H. North, June 2, 1925: I went to Washington and with two other people stood up, listened to a speech by the President, and received the medal. It was more or less of a function at which 75 or 100 people were present. The medal is big enough to knock a man down, and, I suppose, is actually something to be gratified about.[144]

Left: President
Calvin Coolidge.
Wikimedia.

Below: Honorees,
New York Times,
May 16, 1925.

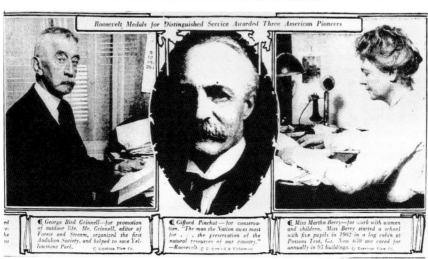

Roosevelt Medals for Distinguished Service Awarded Three American Pioneers

George Bird Grinnell—for promotion of outdoor life. Mr. Grinnell, editor of *Forest and Stream*, organized the first Audubon Society, and helped to save Yellowstone Park. © Keystone View Co.

Gifford Pinchot — for conservation. "The man the Nation owes most for . . . the preservation of the natural resources of our country." —Roosevelt. © Underwood & Underwood

Miss Martha Berry—for work with women and children. Miss Berry started a school with five pupils in 1902 in a log cabin at Possom Trot, Ga. Now 650 are cared for annually in 95 buildings. © Keystone View Co.

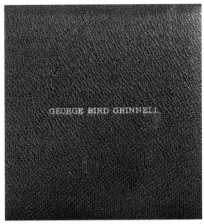

Left: Theodore Roosevelt "For Distinguished Service" Medal, four inches in diameter, three-eighths of an inch thickness, solid gold. *Yale Peabody Museum, author photo.*

Right: Medal case. *Yale Peabody Museum, author photo.*

GLACIER PARK[145]

August 27, 1925

Took the stage along the east shore [of Flathead Lake] to Kalispell....Ticket to Glacier Park $4. Arrived 9:10 P.M.

August 29, 1925

Saw Schultz and wife, Curly Bear (Chief of Piegans) and Jack Monroe at St. Mary's....Jack is sanguinous about his mine....Talked with Curly Bear of various Piegan troubles. It seems a shame that the P's have never been paid anything for the game and timber rights guaranteed them by the treaty of 1895 and taken from them when the park was established.

August 30, 1925

Goodbye to Jack and Schultz. Returned to hotel just after 2 o'c. That night train to Belton.

September 1–11, 1925

In Yellowstone Park. On 9/3 rode horse 6-7 hrs, again on 9/4. Hip bones cut into skin so that I was sore and some blood shows on my drawers. One longs for a woman's strong cushions to sit on.

September 14, 1925

NYC. Met by E., glad to get home.[146]

Among thousands who visited GNP during the recent season, one man to whom the Park meant more because it was the child of his brain, a child that was conceived nearly 35 years ago, but which was not born until 19 years later and which is just now developing into one of the most lusty of the family of National parks, was George Bird Grinnell.... [I]t was due to his untiring energy in fostering and pushing this idea that it finally became a reality.... [I]t was Grinnell's name which was bestowed by others upon three of the most prominent features of the park, Grinnell Mountain, Grinnell Glacier and Grinnell Lake. And last summer when Mr. Grinnell, then 76 years of age, came back into the park, he was merely returning to the bosom of his family, a family of rugged peaks, pine forests, snow banks, beautiful lakes, and old Indians—friends of long ago.[147]

16

1926

Last Visit

JUNE 26

To Chicago, Omaha, Sheridan, Crow Agency, Billings. Elizabeth ill.

JULY 4

To Great Falls.

JULY 5

Browning. Taken by Schultz to Medicine Lodge Camp. Long Talk with Two Guns about treaty of 1895 and hunting, fishing and cutting timber "subject to the laws of Montana."

JULY 6

Talk with Jack, Schultz who gave me copy of last book, Signposts of Adventure. It has much good stuff in it, but some mistakes.
~As mistakenly written in his book, Schultz places Yellowfish and himself on the 1885 hunting trip and states that Grinnell shot a huge ram with horns the size of

washtubs. In fact, Schultz and Yellowfish remained in camp while Grinnell was led by two Kootenai braves. He later shot a two-year-old ewe on the mountain later named Singleshot Mountain by Schultz. The only part of Schultz's story that is true is that Grinnell felled the sheep with a single shot.~

July 9

Riding toward Mt. Henry.

July 11

Arrived Many Glacier (Hotel) about 5 o'c and was given a noisy room by the boys acting as room clerks.

July 12

Met Dr. Elrod....Talked long in the pm with him and found him interesting. Hope to go up on glacier with him, for he is very familiar with it. A Princeton geological party arrives at Entrance on Tuesday and Elrod is to meet them. He is due here again on Wednesday and proposes trip to glacier for the next day.

July 13

Rode up under my mt. along N. side of Lake Josephine to my lake and return. The glacier is melting very fast and the amount of water coming from it is great. All these glaciers are receding rapidly and after a time will disappear....Dr. Elrod suggested that we go to glacier tomorrow. Mr. Noble (GNRR) wishes to go. Much talk about going there in my company. Why?

July 14

About 11 o'c started for glacier. Mr. and Mrs. Noble, Mrs. Binder, Miss Kenney, E. and I. The ride and walk up to the ice as usual. Much of the

Hiking party. *Archives and Special Collections, Mansfield Library, University of Montana, Elrod Photo.*

ice from 3 years ago is gone....Near a stream just above the foot of the moraine saw a mother ptarmigan with one young which already has some feathers. Elrod photographed it and it was so gentle that they tried to put their hands on it. She would not quite stand this. On up the moraine and onto the ice which is covered with slush and running water. The Swiss guide Hans (Riess) had been coming down off ice with another party and Elrod asked him to go back with us. He did so and when we got on ice he roped us together—all except Elrod. We wandered to the wall rock, formerly covered with ice and then along the length of the glacier, which is still an immense mass of ice. Then we went down across crevasses, saw an ice cave....and back to the trail down the moraine. Below we found a Dr. Gastler engaged in photographing the ptarmigan. He made a dozen exposures, he said. With him was Mr. Hall of Cal, the chief naturalist for all Nat'l Parks. By this time I was very leg weary and fell down twice. Everybody was sympathetic about my progress, especially Mrs Binder. After reaching the horses we had some coffee and ate part of the lunch left here when we started up, and half an hour later mounted to return. Trotted all the way back, reaching hotel about 9 pm.

JULY 15

A bad night not withstanding my fatigue of yesterday. All the others seem well and happy....Sat about all morning.

JULY 16

Goodbye to Elrod and Hans. To GP hotel. Saw Monroe's wife at Jack's cabin on way down. Jack not there.

JULY 17

Talked with Mr. Hall, interest in National Parks as educational institutions.... Elrod has a plan for a G.P. Museum building to be built by private subscription.

JULY 18

E. still ill.

JULY 19

News of fires at Lake Josephine and Lake McDonald. Left for East.[148]

— —

After returning to New York, I sent a letter to Dr. Elrod, thanking him for the photographs sent to me, especially "the picture that shows the old ptarmigan and her young one on the rocks by the stream which runs down the moraine. [Making your acquaintance was] the most interesting and pleasant event of my trip to Glacier Park this year. I most enjoyed your small museum at Many Glacier Hotel."[149]

Morton Elrod responded, "I had the pleasure and honor of taking Dr. George Bird Grinnell on a visit to Grinnell Glacier. Although he is 76 years old, yet he went easily over the glacier, to the 'well' at the falls from the upper glacier, across the main ice mass, and back down the trail to the horses."[150]

George Bird Grinnell's Last Visit. *Archives and Special Collections, Mansfield Library, University of Montana, Elrod Photo.*

17

1927–1938

Last Years

I have had barrels of fun! In fact I suspect that there is no one living who ever had so good a time during his life. I remember lodges pitched on the plains— camps by the Republican River, the Platte, the Loup, the Running Water, the Missouri—where with those friends, red and white, I had hunted and feasted.
—George Bird Grinnell

Letter from Robert Sterling Yard, Executive Secretary, National Park Association, to GBG, April 23, 1927: So some of us are thinking that it should have for president, not a scholar, however great, but a man whose name means preservation of nature. We have now the man whose name is greatest for precisely that, whose career goes back to the beginning of nature conservation, who originated every essential thing we stand for, and whose sympathies cover the entire field. [Of course, Yard was writing about GBG.][151]

Letter from Inez L. Ponsche to GBG, August 29, 1927: Greetings to the Father of Glacier National Park....My Brownie snapped this view while we hiked to Grinnell Glacier and I want to send it onto you as a slight token of appreciation for having founded this noble wonderland for us.[152]

~George Bird Grinnell suffered a heart attack at his home in New York in July 1929. Although the initial prognosis was grim, he recovered slowly. Age and persistent illness kept Grinnell in the East during his final years.~

Letter from J.B. Monroe to GBG, December 24, 1933: We went over the St. Mary's Lake-McDonald Lake Auto Road last fall, and it is great. You can now go in an auto, sleep in a feather bed, and live in a steam-heated room on most of our old campgrounds. Better come out and take a real pleasure trip and bid the scenes of our youth "good-bye."[153]

Schultz, *Blackfeet and Buffalo*:

In time he [Grinnell] *became an honorary member of four Plains Indian Tribes. Fisher Hat, as the Blackfeet named him, has done more for them than all the different "Indian Rights", "Indian Aid" societies put together, including getting rid of thieving agents and recommending good ones; helped the Blackfeet get full value for the lands they needed to sell; accompanied their delegates to Washington; and stood by them in their petitions to the Indian Office.*[154]

George Bird Grinnell on "His" Glacier. *Grinnell Family Association of America.*

Bird Grinnell's *New York Times* obituary read as follows:

DR. G.B. GRINNELL, NATURALIST, DEAD
Founder of the First Audubon Society and an Explorer and Author Was 88
April 12, 1938, Tuesday
Dr. George Bird Grinnell, author, naturalist and explorer, who often was called "The Father of American Conservation," died early yesterday at his home, 285 East Fifteenth Street, in his eighty-ninth year. He was a Brooklyn-born easterner who had made 40 trips to the American West and had become a respected authority on the Plains Indians.

Aside from Grinnell's prophetic vision, his forthrightness, his scholarship in the fields of zoology and Indian ethnography, and the drive that empowered him to carry so many causes to successful conclusion, his outstanding personal characteristic was that of never-failing dignity, which was doubtless parcel of all the rest. To meet his eye, feel his iron handclasp, or hear his calm and thrifty words—even when he was a man in his ninth decade—was to conclude that here was the noblest Roman of them all.[155]

As you will see by enclosures, Pinutoyi 'Tsimokan is no more. He was my good friend, a real man![156]

Appendix

GEOLOGICAL FEATURES NAMED
BY GEORGE BIRD GRINNELL

1885

Rose Basin, Creek
Otu Komi Mountain, Lake and Creek
Wilbur Mountain

Swiftcurrent Lake*
Point Mountain
Natahki Lake

*Renamed Lake McDermott in 1889 and subsequently renamed Swiftcurrent Lake in 1929.

1887[†]

Cataract Creek
Gould Mountain
Appekunny Mountain

Grinnell Lake[‡]
Monroe's Peak

[†]1887: Grinnell Glacier and Mountain (named by Lieutenant John H. Beacom, US Army); Grinnell Trail and Point, Fisher Cap Lake (named by USGS topographers)

[‡]Named by Grinnell, Monroe and Appekunny

1888

Four Bears Mountain (Mahtotopa)
Little Chief Mountain
Siyeh Mountain, Glacier, Lake and Creek

Almost-A-Dog Mountain
Citadel Mountain
Almost-A-Boy Mountain

1890

Swiftcurrent Mountain and Glacier
Blackfoot Mountain and Glacier

Iceberg Lake

1891

Allen Mountain
Stimson Mountain and Glacier
Gunsight Mountain, Pass and Lake
Cataract Mountain
Norris Mountain

Seward Mountain
Reynolds Mountain
Jackson Mountain
Fusillade Mountain

1897

The Garden Wall

Harrison Glacier

1898

Cleveland Mountain

ACKNOWLEDGEMENTS

This book could not have been completed without the assistance of friends, both new and old. I want to thank the staffs of the University of Montana, especially Donna McCrea, archivist; Montana State University library staff; Glacier National Park Service, with special kudos to Jean Tabbert, archivist, and Anya Helsel, librarian; Glacier USGS (Lisa McKeon); Autry Museum (Liza Posas); Seward House Museum (Matthew MacVittie); University of Arizona Library staff; Yale University Manuscripts and Archives Library staff; Montana Agricultural Center librarian for introducing me to *Forest and Stream* articles in 2010; Blake Passmore and Ron Casey for enhancing my photographs collection; John Reiger and Richard Vaughn who early on inspired my research; The History Press staff, especially Artie Crisp and Abigail Fleming for critical suggestions that polished this book; John Taliaferro for friendship and encouragement and for writing the "right-on!" foreword in this book; and my wife, Jacquie, for encouragement and keeping me focused on this project.

NOTES

1. James Willard Schultz, *Blackfeet and Buffalo* (Norman: University of Oklahoma Press, 1962), 83.
2. "Apikuni means 'a badly tanned robe which has white hard spots in it.' 'Ap' means white and 'pikuni' is an old name for clothing." Letter from Grinnell to L.O. Vaught, March 14, 1919.
3. George C. Ruhle, *Guide to Glacier National Park* (Minneapolis, MN: Campbell-Mithun Inc., 1949).
4. To the Walled-In Lakes (series), "Up Milk River Valley," *Forest and Stream*, December 10, 1885.
5. Grinnell's daily journal [hereafter daily journal].
6. George Bird Grinnell [hereafter Grinnell], "Some Autumn Birds," *Forest and Stream*, May 24, 1888.
7. Daily journal.
8. "Up Milk River Valley."
9. Daily journal.
10. To the Walled-In Lakes, "Inside Big Waters," *Forest and Stream*, December 17, 1885.
11. Daily journal.
12. To the Walled-In Lakes, "On a Mountainside," *Forest and Stream*, December 24, 1885.
13. Daily journal.
14. Ibid.
15. To the Walled-In Lakes, "Lazy Days," *Forest and Stream*, December 31, 1885.
16. Daily journal.

17. Ibid.
18. To the Walled-In Lakes, "Hunting with the Kootenays," *Forest and Stream*, January 7, 1886.
19. Daily journal, September 10, 1885.
20. Daily journal.
21. To the Walled-In Lakes, "Big Fish on Little Rod," *Forest and Stream*, January 28, 1886.
22. To the Walled-In Lakes, "Night In the Lodge," *Forest and Stream*, February 4, 1886.
23. To the Walled-In Lakes, "Up Swift Current," *Forest and Stream*, February 11, 1886.
24. Ruhle, *Guide to Glacier National Park*.
25. "Up Swift Current."
26. To the Walled-In Lakes, "A Portent of Evil," *Forest and Stream*, February 18, 1886.
27. To the Walled-In Lakes, "Goat Hunting and Grumbling," *Forest and Stream*, February 25, 1886.
28. To the Walled-In Lakes, "Plenty Horses Stolen," *Forest and Stream*, March 4, 1886.
29. To the Walled-In Lakes, "A Bear Pipe Dance," *Forest and Stream*, March 11, 1886.
30. To the Walled-In Lakes, "A Christening," *Forest and Stream*, March 18, 1886.
31. Grinnell, "Audubon Society," *Forest and Stream*, February 25, 1886.
32. John G. Mitchell, "A Man Called Bird," *Audubon*, March 1987, 94–98.
33. Ibid.
34. Ibid.
35. Grinnell, "Hunting Trips of a Ranchman," *Forest and Stream*, July 2, 1885.
36. Douglas Brinkley, *The Wilderness Warrior: Theodore Roosevelt and the Crusade for America*, chapter 7, "Cradle of Conservation: The Elkhorn Ranch of North Dakota," Erenow.net.
37. University of Montana Archives, box 1, folder 4.
38. Brinkley, *Wilderness Warrior*, chapter 8, "Wildlife Protection Business: Boone and Crockett Club," Erenow.net.
39. Grinnell, "Boone and Crockett Club," *Forest and Stream*, January 17, 1889.
40. Grinnell, "By St. Mary Lakes," *Forest and Stream*, December 29, 1887.
41. Grinnell, "Whiskey Trader's Camp," *Forest and Stream*, January 12, 1888.
42. Richard Vaughn, "To the Ice," *Journal of the West* 49, no. 1 (Winter 2010): 14.
43. Grinnell, "The Naming of the Tribes," *Forest and Stream*, January 19, 1888.

44. Grinnell, "Fruitless Clambering," *Forest & Stream*, January 26, 1888.

45. Daily journal.

46. Grinnell, "A Piece of Meat," *Forest and Stream*, February 8, 1888.

47. Grinnell, "Piece of Meat," 8.

48. Grinnell, "Facing a Blizzard," *Forest and Stream*, February 23, 1888.

49. Grinnell, "Storm Bound," *Forest and Stream*, March 1, 1888.

50. Daily journal.

51. Grinnell, "A Night Ride," *Forest and Stream*, March 15, 1888.

52. Daily journal.

53. Grinnell, "Hunting a Glacier," *Forest and Stream*, March 22, 1888.

54. Ibid.

55. Letter to GBG from M.W. Beacom, April 30, 1917, with the page transcribed from John Beacom's diary, University of Montana Archives.

56. Daily journal.

57. Grinnell, "Hunting a Glacier."

58. Daily journal.

59. Grinnell, "A River of Ice," *Forest and Stream*, March 29, 1888.

60. Ibid.

61. Daily journal.

62. Grinnell, "River of Ice."

63. Daily journal.

64. Grinnell, "River of Ice."

65. Grinnell, "Visitors to the Camp," *Forest and Stream*, April 19, 1888.

66. The name *Appekunny Mountain* was later transferred to another mountain north of fourth lake. The remaining mountain is Grinnell Mountain, and the former Appekunny Mountain is Grinnell Point.

67. Grinnell, "Packers and Harness Makers," *Forest and Stream*, April 26, 1888.

68. Daily journal.

69. Grinnell, "Packers and Harness Makers."

70. Grinnell, "Misfortunes of Pani Puk'koats," *Forest and Stream*, December 6, 1888.

71. Daily journal.

72. Grinnell, Slide Rock from Many Mountains (series), no. 10, "On a Glacier in Summer," *Forest and Stream*, October 10, 1890.

73. Grinnell, "Misfortunes of Pani Puk'koats."

74. Daily journal.

75. Grinnell, Slide Rock from Many Mountains, no. 4, "Meat in the Pot," *Forest and Stream*, March 6, 1890.

76. Grinnell, "Misfortunes of Pani Puk'koats."

77. Daily journal.

78. Schultz, *Blackfeet and Buffalo*, 96.
79. C.W. Buckholtz, *Man in Glacier* (Glacier Natural History Association, 1976). "Following some escalating incidents between the Blackfeet and some whites near Ft. Benton and Helena, an early Montana settler, Malcolm Clark, was killed by some Piegan, and the demand for immediate retaliation echoed throughout the territory. Major Eugene M. Baker was dispatched to punish the offending Indians. Instead of finding the hostiles in a camp led by Mountain Chief, Baker encountered a camp of smallpox-stricken Piegan led by Heavy Runner and attacked them, killing 173 of the Indians, fifty-three of whom were women and children. This controversial 'Baker Massacre' ended organized Indian resistance along Montana's front range."
80. Daily journal.
81. Daily journal.
82. Yale Archives, George Bird Grinnell Papers, MS1388, reel 3.
83. Smithsonian Archives.
84. University of Montana Mansfield Library, Connecticut Audubon Society microfilm, reel 2.
85. Daily journal.
86. "Crown of the Continent," *Century Magazine*, September 1, 1901, 671.
87. Daily journal.
88. Warren L. Hanna, *Life and Times of J. W. Schultz* (Norman: University of Oklahoma Press, 1986), 171–73.
89. University of Montana Mansfield Library, Connecticut Audubon Society microfilm, reel 2.
90. GBG untitled, unpublished article, August 2, 1928 to August 6, 1928, George Bird Grinnell Papers (MS 1388), Yale Manuscripts and Archives.
91. University of Montana Archives, Grinnell Collection, box 3, folder 1.
92. Ibid., box 3, folder 22.
93. Seward practiced law his whole life. Stimson became a statesman and was secretary of state for President Hoover and later secretary of war for Presidents Franklin Roosevelt and Harry Truman.
94. University of Montana Archives, Grinnell Collection, box 3, folder 1.
95. GBG untitled, unpublished article (see n. 90).
96. Hanna, *Life and Times of James Willard Schultz*, 172.
97. Yale University, reel 23, William H. Seward letter to GBG, March 1, 1918.
98. Unknown to Bird Grinnell, in 1832, George Catlin proposed a national park, and in 1883, Lieutenant Van Orsdale suggested "the entire area encompassed by these mountains be set aside into a national park."
99. Hanna, *Life and Times of James Willard Schultz*, 17.

100. Yale University, reel 23, William H. Seward letter to GBG, March 1, 1918.

101. Letter from GBG to J.B. Monroe, February 25, 1892, Yale Manuscripts and Archives.

102. GBG unpublished article, August 2, 1928 to August 6, 1928, George Bird Grinnell Papers (MS 1388), Yale Manuscripts and Archives.

103. University of Montana Archives, box 1, folder 10.

104. University of Montana Archives, box 1, folder 12 (1895 Letters).

105. Christopher S. Ashby, "Blackfeet Agreement of 1895 and Glacier National Park, A Case History" (master's thesis, University of Montana, 1985).

106. Daily journal.

107. Ashby, "Blackfeet Agreement of 1895."

108. Daily journal.

109. Ashby, "Blackfeet Agreement of 1895."

110. Ibid.

111. Daily journal.

112. University of Montana Archives, Connecticut Audubon Society microfilm, reels 6/7.

113. Donald H. Robinson, *Through the Years in Glacier National Park* (Whitefish, MT: Sun Point Press, 1960).

114. University of Montana Archives, Connecticut Audubon Society, reel 10.

115. "Climbing Blackfoot," *Forest and Stream*, October 8, 1898.

116. *Century Magazine*, September 1901.

117. 1901 letters, University of Montana Archives, box 1, folder 18.

118. 1902 and 1903 letters, University of Montana Library, Connecticut Audubon Society (CAS) microfilm, reels 2, 8, 9.

119. *Auk, Quarterly Journal of Ornithology* (January 1939).

120. Daily journal.

121. Gifford Pinchot, U.S. Forest Service.

122. University of Montana Archives, Grinnell Correspondence Files, box 1, folder 24.

123. Ibid., GBG letter to Robert Underwood.

124. Ibid., GBG letter to John N. Sharpe, Crow Agency, Montana, March 11, 1908.

125. Ibid., box 2, folder 1.

126. University of Montana, Grinnell Files, Great Northern Railway, *History of Glacier National Park*, 1960.

127. Southwest Museum, Connecticut Audubon Society microfilm, Grinnell Correspondence Files.

128. University of Montana Archives, 1911–1914 letters, box 2, folder 4.

129. Daily journal.
130. Great Northern Railway, *History of Glacier National Park.*
131. Michael J. Ober, *Glacier Album* (Helena, MT: Riverbend Publishing, 2010), 29.
132. Ibid.
133. University of Montana Archives, 1912, 1913, 1914 letters, box 2, folder 5, 6, 7.
134. Ibid.
135. Daily journal.
136. Ibid.
137. Glacier NPS, Letters from Grinnell and Vaught collections.
138. Grinnell Family Association newsletter, "Interview with Mrs. George B. Grinnell" [June 19, 1956], author's collection.
139. Daily journal.
140. Yale University Manuscripts and Archives.
141. Daily journal.
142. Glacier NPS Archives, L.O. Vaught Collection.
143. Speech quoted from *New York Times*, May 16, 1925, Yale University Manuscripts and Archives.
144. University of Montana Archives, Connecticut Audubon Society microfilm, reel 29.
145. Ibid.
146. Daily journal.
147. University of Montana Archives, Connecticut Audubon Society microfilm, reel 29.
148. Daily journal.
149. Letter to Morton Elrod, August 6, 1926, University of Montana Archives, Connecticut Audubon Society, reel 29.
150. Elrod, Report of the Park Naturalist, 1926, unpublished except for internal use.
151. Yale University, Manuscripts and Archives, Connecticut Audubon Society microfilm, reel 35.
152. Ibid., reel 36.
153. Ibid., reel 35.
154. Schultz, *Blackfeet and Buffalo.*
155. Yale Manuscripts and Archives.
156. Schultz, letter to his son, Hart Merriam Schultz, April 15, 1938.

INDEX

ABOUT THE AUTHOR

Hugh Grinnell received his bachelor's and master's degrees from the University of Arizona. Since his retirement in 2004, Hugh has studied the history of the Great American West. After discovering an old Great Northern Railway passenger car named Grinnell Glacier, he researched the name to discover that the glacier was named to honor the efforts of George Bird Grinnell, a distant cousin, to preserve the area. As a member of the Great Northern Railway Historical Society, Hugh was invited to present "Saving the Great American West" (the life of George Bird Grinnell) to the attendees at their 2010 Annual Convention, in Glacier National Park, on the occasion of the 100th anniversary of the creation of the park. The Great Northern Railway Historical Society published several historical articles written by Hugh about the railroad. While president (2005–10) of the Grinnell Family (genealogy) Association of America, he also wrote and produced a DVD that profiles twelve important Grinnells in American history. George Bird Grinnell is foremost among these.

Hugh is the great-grandson of Herbert Balcom Grinnell, one of the three founders of Grinnell Brothers Music House in Michigan in 1880. By the 1960s, Grinnell Brothers had become the largest music company in the world, boasting the largest collection of published music and selling more pianos (including Steinway) than any other company. As a teenager in the Tucson Arizona Boys Chorus from 1951 to 1955, Hugh appeared on *The Ed Sullivan Show* and toured Canada, forty U.S. states and seven European countries. In 1968, he was in the backup group that accompanied Bill

Medley on his new release, "Peace, Brother, Peace!," which was premiered on the Smothers Brothers TV show. Hugh studied piano and sang in several professional chorales in California (1960s–1980s). He sings in the St. Mark Church choir in Oro Valley, Arizona.

Hugh is also a public speaker, presenting a one-hour condensed version taken from this book. He first presented this program at the 2010 Grinnell Family reunion in Providence, Rhode Island, and has since spoken on this topic in both Montana and Arizona more than seventy times, including ten programs inside Glacier National Park.